CAS AUG 2000 X

OFFICIALLY WITHDRAWN
FROM NORTH CENTRAL REGIONAL
LIBRARY COLLECTION

D0473691

BLACK & DECKER®

THE COMPLETE GUIDE TO

HOME MASONRY

C5

Step-by-Step
Projects & Repairs
Using Concrete, Brick, Block & Stone

CREATIVE
PUBLISHING
international

MINNETONKA, MINNESOTA

NORTH CENTRAL REGIONAL LIBRARY
Headquarters Wenatchee WA

Contents

CREATIVE
PUBLISHING
international

Copyright © 2000
Creative Publishing international, Inc.
5900 Green Oak Drive
Minnetonka, Minnesota 55343
1-800-328-3895
All rights reserved

Printed in America by:
Quebecor World
10 9 8 7 6 5 4 3 2 1

President/CEO: David D. Murphy
Vice President/Editor-in-Chief: Patricia K. Jacobsen
Vice President/Retail Sales & Marketing: Richard M. Miller

Executive Editor: Bryan Trandem
Creative Director: Tim Himsel
Managing Editor: Michelle Skudlarek
Editorial Director: Jerri Farris

Lead Editor: Daniel London
Editors: Paul Currie, Phil Schmidt
Copy Editor: Jennifer Caliandro
Senior Art Director: Kevin Walton
Mac Designers: Kari Johnston, Jon Simpson
Technical Photo Editor: Keith Thompson
Technical Photo Assistants: Sean T. Doyle, Christopher Kennedy
Assisting Project Manager: Julie Caruso
Technical Reader: Lee Mosman
Photo Researcher: Angela Hartwell
Studio Services Manager: Marcia Chambers
Studio Services Coordinator: Carol Osterhus
Photo Team Leader: Chuck Nields
Photographers: Andrea Rugg, Rebecca Schmidt, Joel Schnell
Scene Shop Carpenters: Scott Ashfield, David O. Johnson,
  Greg Wallace, Dan Widerski
Director of Production Services: Kim Gerber
Production Manager: Helga Thielen

THE COMPLETE GUIDE TO HOME MASONRY
Created by: The Editors of Creative Publishing international, Inc.,
in cooperation with Black & Decker. BLACK & DECKER is a trademark
of The Black & Decker Corporation and is used under license

Masonry Projects

Masonry Repairs

Library of Congress
Cataloging-in-Publication Data

The complete guide to home masonry :
step-by-step projects & repairs using concrete, brick, block & stone / Black & Decker.

p. cm.
Includes index.
ISBN 0-86573-592-1
1. Masonry—Amateurs' manuals. 2.
Dwellings—Maintenance and repair—Amateurs' manuals. I. Black & Decker Corporation (Towson, Md.) II. Creative Publishing
international.

TH5313.C6525 2000
693'.1— dc21
99-057797

Portions of *The Complete Guide to Home Masonry*
are taken from *Home Masonry Repairs & Projects,
Landscape Design & Construction, Building Garden
Ornaments, The Complete Photo Guide to Home
Repair, Carpentry: Remodeling, Everyday Home
Repairs,* and *Building Your Outdoor Home.* Other
titles from Creative Publishing international include:

*The New Everyday Home Repairs, Decorating
With Paint & Wallcovering, Carpentry: Tools •
Shelves • Walls • Doors, Basic Wiring & Electrical
Repairs, Workshop Tips & Techniques, Advanced
Home Wiring, Carpentry: Remodeling, Land-
scape Design & Construction, Bathroom Remod-
eling, Built-In Projects for the Home, Refinishing
& Finishing Wood, Exterior Home Repairs &
Improvements, Home Masonry Repairs & Pro-
jects, Building Porches & Patios, Flooring Pro-
jects & Techniques, Advanced Home Plumbing,
Remodeling Kitchens, The Complete Photo
Guide to Home Repair, The Complete Guide to
Home Plumbing, The Complete Guide to Home
Wiring, The Complete Guide to Decks, The
Complete Guide to Painting & Decorating.*

The Complete Guide
to Home Masonry

Introduction

Step outside and take a look around your home. Masonry materials are around every corner, adding to the beauty and value of your home. From the poured concrete footings to the concrete chimney cap, masonry is one of the essential elements that make your house into a comfortable, safe living environment. The same holds true for your landscaping. You may have a stone retaining wall that shores up your front lawn, a brick-paver driveway to provide a smooth welcome mat for cars and bicycles, or poured concrete steps on which you and your guests have trod countless miles. And when all the elements are in good repair, your house and yard become a source of pride, a neighborhood asset, and an investment that's gaining in value.

As a do-it-yourselfer, you may shy away from building a house foundation—and wisely so—but with a basic set of tools, there is a nearly infinite number of masonry projects you can take on. They range in complexity from creating your own stepping stones to pouring a driveway and building entire walls, pillars, and arches.

Why is masonry so appealing? In addition to its remarkable strength, it has striking reflective qualities that distinguish it from wood construction. The "look" of masonry can range from the ruddy tones of adobe bricks to the mottled hues of a cut stone such as granite. Masonry often contains pebbles and smaller "aggregates" that glimmer when wet or in direct sunlight and have an equally distinctive look in the shade. The range of possibilities means you can use masonry to complement any garden or landscape. You can also combine masonry with painted and natural wood surfaces, and countless other materials. In this book, we recommend materials that are easy to find at stone and brick yards and home centers. We also introduce you to hypertufa, a masonry material that is excellent for crafting rustic outdoor accessories.

NOTICE TO READERS

This book provides useful instructions, but we cannot anticipate all of your working conditions or the characteristics of your materials and tools. For safety, you should use caution, care, and good judgment when following the procedures described in this book. Consider your own skill level and the instructions and safety precautions associated with the various tools and materials shown. Neither the publisher nor BLACK&DECKER can assume responsibility for any damage to property or injury to persons as a result of misuse of the information provided.

The instructions in this book conform to "The Uniform Plumbing Code," "The National Electrical Code Reference Book," and "The Uniform Building Code" current at the time of its original publication. Consult your local Building Department for information on building permits, codes, and other laws as they apply to your project.

Our goal is to help you learn the fundamentals of masonry construction. Then you can work with just about any masonry material and add beauty and character to your home. We recommend that you start any project by consulting your local building inspector about the Building Code requirements in your area. Meeting these requirements will result in an attractive home improvement that will stand the test of time.

The "Introduction" guides you in planning your projects and selecting tools and materials, so you can get the best results with the least effort.

Section two, "Basic Techniques" (pages 24 to 97), teaches you the basics about each masonry material—concrete, brick, block, stone, stucco, and more—so you can combine time-tested methods with even the latest masonry styles.

Section three, "Masonry Projects" (pages 98 to 237), offers attractive designs and clear, concise plans that we've created with the do-it-yourselfer in mind. You can complete some of these projects yourself in just a few hours. For others, we recommend that you work with a group of friends and plan on spending a few days on the project. Either way, you'll be extremely pleased with the results.

In Section four, "Repairs" (pages 238 to 278), we guide you through just about every home masonry repair suitable for homeowners.

At the back of the book, you can find a list of metric conversions, resources for further research, a glossary of terms used throughout this book, and an index for quickly locating subjects of interest to you.

Good luck, and enjoy! With some planning and attention to detail, your masonry projects can be a source of pride and admiration for many years.

Masonry & Your Home

What's the most important construction material in your home? Your first instinct may be to say that it's the lumber that frames the structure. Think again. Even more essential is the masonry that likely forms your home's foundation. After all, without a strong foundation—and most home foundations are either poured concrete or concrete block—even the best frame won't support your home for long.

Architects and builders determined long ago that nothing competes with masonry's combination of strength, durability, and weather-resistance. That's why your home probably contains more than 35 tons of masonry materials. These materials are not found only in your home's foundation. Take a look around your home and you'll find they're widely used in more visible areas as well, such as exterior brick, stone or stucco walls, clay or concrete tile roofs, and brick or stone chimneys. That's because masonry materials are among the most versatile in blending with all kinds of surroundings.

Take a walk around your yard and garden and you'll quickly appreciate how important masonry is to your outdoor spaces as well. Brick, block, and stone have always been popular for lawn and garden structures, patios, and other paved surfaces.

But today's homeowners are finding more and more outdoor uses for masonry, such as forming planters and other small garden accents with moldable concrete mixtures. In fact, new methods and products have simplified lots of age-old techniques, putting a growing number of projects within your reach.

Anyone who owns a home knows that masonry does require occasional repair and upkeep. While making repairs is not difficult, it is important that you do it with the best repair materials, techniques, and tools. A poorly planned and executed masonry repair will look like a glaring mistake. Good repair work will blend in so well it can go virtually unnoticed.

The following pages are designed to show you the range of possibilities as you begin to think about masonry projects for your home. "Planning & Designing Masonry Projects" (pages 12 to 15) guides you through the process of preparing for and completing your project carefully so you get the most out of your results.

Common Masonry Projects

Steps and walkways are among the most popular masonry projects. A well-designed walkway may be a series of concrete slabs and steps that take you from your doorstep to the sidewalk, driveway, or garage. Or, it may be a narrow stepping-stone path that meanders through your garden.

(continued page 10)

Patios are simple to lay—whether finished with tile, concrete, brick pavers, or other materials. Yards with patios often get more use because the finished space beckons homeowners outdoors for meals and socializing as well as gardening and recreation.

A masonry wall—whether built out of stone, brick, or block—can create a sense of privacy, muffle neighborhood noise, or divide an expansive lawn into more intimate and manageable spaces. Adding a gate or arch turns a wall into a threshold from one part of your property to the next.

Masonry lends itself to more than just large-scale paving and wall construction. Hypertufa, a type of concrete that incorporates peat moss, is ideal for molding into planters, birdbaths, and other creations that can add the perfect accent to your yard.

An arch makes a spectacular addition to any entryway. A pair of freestanding brick or stone walls makes the perfect opening. Using a curved plywood form, you can assemble an arch in a matter of hours.

The moon window is one of the most striking and unusual types of archwork. Full-scale "walk-through" moon gates are a challenge to construct. Yet it's not difficult to build one on a modest scale like the example above.

A retaining wall is first and foremost a means of holding back earth on a sloped yard. It's also an excellent way to terrace a sloped yard to create planting beds or other landscaping options that dramatically alter the look of a yard or garden.

Outdoor tile is an ideal material for dressing up a concrete patio that's old and cracked. By first pouring a fresh concrete subbase over the existing slab, you ensure that problems in the original slab won't affect your newly installed tile.

Test project layouts by using a rope or hose to outline proposed project areas. This will help you make decisions about size, scale, and shape. For curved walkways, use spacers between the borders of the project site to maintain an accurate, even width.

Planning & Designing Masonry Projects

There are two basic stages to planning and designing any masonry building project. First, gather creative ideas to help plan a project that is both practical and attractive. Second, apply the basic standards of masonry construction to your idea to create a plan that is structurally sound and complies with the local Building Code.

One of the best ways to acquire design ideas is simply to take casual walks through your neighborhood. Bring along a notebook and record your observations about the masonry structures or surfaces you see. There is no better way to know what a design will look like than to see a similar project in completed form.

Good masonry takes into account size and scale, location, slope and drainage, reinforcement, material selection, and appearance. All of the tips and information on the following pages are designed to help familiarize you with these design elements.

If you do not have much masonry experience, start with simple, stand-alone projects. Building a small garden wall or pouring a short backyard walkway are good first-time projects. Repairing existing structures also provides valuable experience for future building projects.

Tips for Designing a Masonry Project

Build a three-dimensional mock-up when planning a wall or other tall structure using tall stakes, mason's string, and landscape fabric, packing paper, or plastic. View the mock structure from all sides to get a sense of how it will obstruct views and access, and how it will blend with other landscape elements.

Make detailed plan drawings. By using graph paper to create scaled drawings of the planned project, you can eliminate design flaws and make better estimates of building material requirements. In some cases, local codes may require you to obtain a permit before beginning the project, and scaled plan drawings usually are needed for permit approval. Always check with your local building department early in the planning process.

Common Masonry Projects Around the Home

Project	Level of Difficulty	Special Considerations
Decorative Accents (planters, birdbaths, home-made stepping stones, etc.)	Basic to Moderate	Good projects for beginners. Simple projects with few structural requirements. Most can be completed in a few hours.
Walkways & Paths	Basic to Moderate	Square corners are simple to create; curves and angles complicate the project. Walkways are subject to codes that govern size, reinforcement, location, and allowable materials. Often built adjacent to other permanent structures, creating a need for isolation joints.
Brick, Block & Stone Walls	Basic to Advanced	Simple garden-type walls are easy to build; project difficulty increases with size, complexity of stacking pattern, and need for reinforcement. Walls over 3 ft. tall generally require frost footings; wall caps or free-end pillars may be needed.
Patios	Moderate to Advanced	Large surface areas require the use of control joints and isolation joints. Large volume of concrete requires very efficient placing and finishing techniques; can be broken down into several small projects with the use of permanent forms. Establishing slope can be tricky.
Driveways & Garage Floors	Advanced	Subbase preparation and grading are important and time-consuming. Can require special tools, such as a bull float, to handle large volume of concrete. High-strength concrete often required. Garage floors often steel-floated for a hard, semi-gloss surface.
Arches & Moon Windows	Advanced	Curved surfaces typically require more cutting of bricks or stones and a curved plywood form for construction. Special care is required to avoid strain or injury while positioning the materials.

(continued next page)

Tips for Designing a Masonry Project (continued)

Bring home samples of the materials you have in mind so you can see first-hand how they will look on-site. Cumbersome as it may be to cart rock or concrete block, it is worth the extra effort to be able to look over different textures and colors alongside your house, garden, and other landscaping elements.

Many suppliers provide sample boards (below left) so you can avoid carrying home large, bulky materials. Ask for mortar tint samples (below right) as well, so you can decide which tint goes best with the other materials you've selected.

Not every masonry material is appropriate for every climate. It is no surprise that deeply textured bricks such as adobe are more common in regions where winter weather is less harsh. Some may include compounds designed to make them more weather-resistant, but textured brick is much like recycled brick (taken from demolished buildings)—it has an appealing aged look, but also has more places for water to permeate. Water is generally harmless in warm climates, but can cause damage if the temperature often falls below 32°F. Even small amounts of water expand when it freezes, resulting in major cracking. A local supplier can point out materials that are recommended in your region.

Check drainage. Good drainage lets water percolate through the crushed rock or topsoil on your property, draining puddles on the surface. It allows a stepping stone path to shed water quickly after a storm, and keeps concrete slabs from buckling due to freeze-thaw cycles. Soil that contains clay or is compacted may not drain well. If you notice standing water on your lawn long after a storm, it is a sign of a problem. Test the drainage by digging a hole roughly 4" in diameter by 12" deep and filling the hole with water. Let the water drain. If water remains after 24 hours, drainage is inadequate.

Ask a local landscaper how you can improve the soil before starting your masonry project. When pouring a slab, the solution is often simple: Lay plastic sheets along the base of the site (page 26) to create an effective water barrier.

Home centers carry the materials and tools you will need for most masonry projects. Many brick yards and stone suppliers also carry a wide range of specialty tools that can simplify your projects.

Estimating & Ordering Materials

Whether you are pouring a small slab or building an archway, estimate the dimensions of your project as accurately as possible. You will eliminate extra shopping trips and delivery costs.

Use the estimating chart (page 17) to determine how much of each masonry material you need. Since it is difficult to estimate these quantities exactly, add 10 percent to your estimate for each item. This will help you anticipate small oversights and allow for for waste when cutting.

If you are building with brick, a local brick yard is where you'll find the best supply of bricklayer's materials. They can offer professional advice and

often carry tools and other materials. The same goes for suppliers of natural stone.

Masonry tools, and materials such as concrete, mortar, and stucco mix, caulks, repair compounds, and metal fasteners, are available at home centers. However, you should consider the scale of your project before purchasing concrete or stucco by the bag. For large projects, such as a patio or driveway, you may want to hire a ready-mix supplier (page 45) to deliver fresh concrete. Just remember, you will need a team of friends and plenty of tools on hand when the concrete arrives. With concrete and other troweled masonry, timing is critical.

How to Estimate Materials

Sand, gravel, topsoil (2" layer)	surface area (sq. ft.) ÷ 100 = tons needed
Standard brick pavers for walks and patios (4" × 8")	surface area (sq. ft.) × 5 = number of pavers needed
Standard bricks for walls and pillars (4" × 8")	surface area (sq. ft.) × 7 = number of bricks needed (single brick thickness)
Poured concrete (4" layer)	surface area (sq. ft.) × .012 = cubic yards needed
Flagstone	surface area (sq. ft.) ÷ 100 = tons of stone needed
Interlocking Block (6" × 16" face)	area of wall face (sq. ft.) × 1.5 = number of stones needed
Ashlar stone for 1-ft.-thick walls	area of wall face (sq. ft.) ÷ 15 = tons of stone needed
Rubble stone for 1-ft.-thick walls	area of wall face (sq. ft.) ÷ 35 = tons of stone needed
8" × 8" × 16" concrete block for freestanding walls	height of wall (ft.) × length of wall × 1.125 = number of blocks needed

Use this chart to estimate the materials you will need. Sizes and weights of materials may vary, so consult your supplier for more detailed information. The availability and cost of gravel and stone products vary from region to region. Visit a stone supplier to see the products firsthand. When sand, gravel, and other bulk materials are delivered, place them on a tarp to protect your yard. Make sure the tarp is as close to your work area as possible.

Local brick and stone suppliers will often help you design your project and advise you about estimating materials, local Building Codes, and climate considerations. Many suppliers offer a range of other services as well, such as coordinating landscapers and other contractors to work with you and offering classes in masonry construction.

Tools for mixing concrete and for site preparation include: a sturdy wheelbarrow (A) with a minimum capacity of 6 cubic ft.; power concrete mixer (B) for large poured concrete projects (more than ½-1 cubic yard); masonry hoe (C) and mortar box (D) for mixing mortar and small amounts of concrete; square-end spade (E) for removing sod by hand, excavating, and settling poured concrete; and tamper (F) for compacting the building site and subbase. Also shown: a sod cutter (G) for stripping sod for reuse.

Masonry Tools & Equipment

To work effectively with masonry products, you will need to buy or rent some special-purpose tools. Trowels, floats, edgers, and jointers are hand tools used to place, shape, and finish concrete and mortar. Chisels are used to cut and fit brick and block. Equip your circular saw and power drill with blades designed for use with concrete and brick to convert them into special-purpose masonry tools.

Successfully mixing concrete and mortar also depends on good tool selection. For most poured concrete projects, a power concrete mixer is a valuable tool. If the project requires more than one cubic yard of concrete (see chart, page 17), have pre-mixed concrete delivered to save time and back strain, while ensuring a uniform mixing consistency for the entire project. For small concrete or mortar-set projects, use a mortar box and masonry hoe.

Make the layout process easier and more accurate by using the proper alignment and measuring tools (page 19), and make sure you have the necessary safety equipment on hand before you start your project, including gloves and protective eye wear (page 22 to 23).

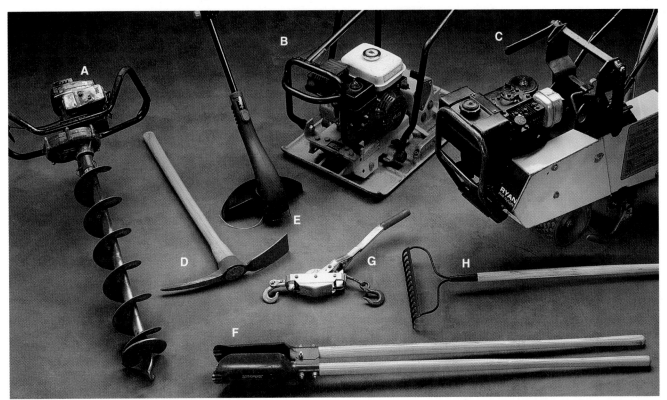

Landscaping tools for preparing sites for masonry projects include: a power auger (A) for digging holes for posts or poles; power tamper (B) and power sod cutter (C) for driveway and other large-scale site preparation. You can easily rent these at a local rental center. You may want to purchase some smaller landscaping tools, including: a pick (D) for exca- vating hard or rocky soil; weed trimmer (E) for removing brush and weeds before digging; posthole digger (F) for when you have just one or two holes to dig; come-along (G) for moving large rocks and other heavy objects without excessive lifting; and garden rake (H) for moving small amounts of soil and debris.

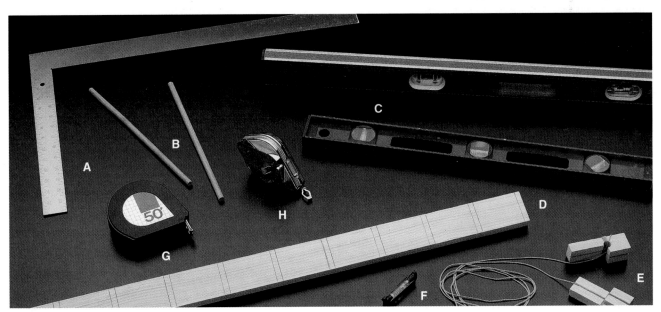

Alignment and measuring tools for masonry projects include: a framing square (A) for setting project outlines; ⅜" dowels (B) for use as spacers between dry-laid masonry units; levels (C) for setting forms and checking stacked masonry units; a story pole (D) that can be calibrated for stacking masonry units; line blocks and mason's string (E) for stacking brick and block; a line level (F) for making layouts and setting slope; a tape measure (G); and a chalk line (H) for marking layout lines on footings or slabs.

(continued next page)

Basic hand and power tools include: a shop broom (A) for keeping your work site clean and for creating a textured surface on poured concrete; bucket and scrub brush (B) for removing dirt and stains; stiff-bristle brushes (C) for cleaning tough stains and removing loose material; hand saw (D) for cutting forms; hacksaw (E) for trimming PVC pipe, rebar, and other materials; rubber mallet (F) for setting brick pavers; reciprocating saw (G) for cutting PVC, rebar, and other materials; crowbar (H) and pry bar (I) for rebuilding stone walls; pipe clamps (J) used when scoring large quantities of brick or block; aviation snips (K) for trimming metal ties and stucco lath; bolt cutters (L) for cutting rebar and wire mesh; circular saw (M) for scoring brick, block, and stone (using a masonry blade) or cutting wood forms (using a combination blade); hammer drill with masonry bit (N) for drilling into masonry; hammer (O) for driving nails into forms; power drill with masonry bit (P) for light drilling in masonry; caulk gun (Q) for sealing around fasteners and house trim; and garden hose with spray nozzle (R) for wetting masonry during curing and cleaning.

Mason's tools include: a darby (A) for smoothing screeded concrete; mortar hawk (B) for holding mortar; pointing trowel (C) for tuck pointing stone mortar; wide pointing tool (D) for tuck pointing or placing mortar on brick and block walls; jointer (E) for finishing mortar joints; brick tongs (F) for carrying multiple bricks; narrow tuck-pointer (G) for tuck-pointing or placing mortar on brick and block walls; mason's trowel (H) for applying mortar; masonry chisels (I) for splitting brick, block, and stone; bullfloat (J) for float-ing large slabs; mason's hammers (K) for chipping brick and stone; maul (L) for driving stakes; square-end trowel (M) for concrete finishing; side edger (N) and step edger (O) for finishing inside and outside corners of concrete; joint chisel (P) for removing dry mortar; control jointer (Q) for creating control joints; tile nippers (R) for trimming tile; sled jointer (S) for smoothing long joints; steel trowel (T) for finishing concrete; magnesium or wood float (U) for floating concrete; screed board (V) for screeding concrete.

Working Safely

Working with masonry requires a variety of precautions to prevent injuries from caustic materials, sharp edges, flying shards of stone, and other materials:

• Wear a particle mask, gloves, and protective eye wear when handling or mixing dry mixes, and follow the manufacturer's safety precautions. Concrete and mortar mixes contain silica, which is hazardous in large quantities and will irritate skin.

• Cutting and sawing masonry materials produces dust and flying particles. A mask, gloves, and protective eye wear are essential when using striking or cutting tools, such as mauls, chisels, and saws.

• Lifting and moving masonry products is hard work. For added protection when lifting, wear a lifting belt and use safe lifting techniques.

• Use a GFCI extension cord for plugging in power tools outdoors or when materials are wet. A GFCI cord protects against electrical shock caused by a faulty tool or a worn or wet cord or plug.

Wear protective equipment, including a particle mask, eye wear, and gloves when mixing masonry products. Concrete products can be health hazards, and they will irritate skin upon contact. Also wear a mask to protect yourself from dust when cutting concrete, brick, or block.

Tips for Working Safely

Wear a lifting belt to help prevent lower back strain when stacking brick and block, and when hand-mixing concrete products. Always lift with your legs, not your back, and keep the items being lifted as close to your body as you can.

Keep the job site clean and well organized by designating a tool area and by sweeping the work site frequently.

Tips for Working at Heights

Anchor your ladder at the top and bottom, using rope and a screw eye at the top, and stakes at the bottom. Do not carry heavy items up ladders—use a rope and pulley.

Use rented scaffolding for projects that require extended time working at heights, such as tuck-pointing a chimney. Scaffolding provides a much safer working platform, and is easier on the legs than a ladder. Get safety and operating instructions from the rental store if you have not used scaffolding before. Always make sure the feet of the scaffolding are level and secure (inset).

Use a GFCI extension cord or outlet any time you run corded power tools outdoors. A GFCI is the best protection against an electrical shock. Always inspect power cords and repair any nicks or cuts before using your power tools.

Use muriatic acid only when stains don't respond to a powdered cleanser. Acid can cause burns, so wear rubber gloves and goggles and work in a well-ventilated area. When diluting acid, always pour acid into water following the manufacturer's mixing guidelines.

Avoiding Drainage Problems

If your yard slopes in the direction of a planned masonry project, or if the soil drains poorly (page 15), take steps to avoid problems in the future. You can eliminate small slopes by filling in low-lying areas with fresh soil. If you're pouring a slab in a poorly drained area, protect the bottom of the slab by covering the ground with 6 mil polyethylene sheeting. For large low-lying areas, dig a drainage swale that will direct water toward a runoff area.

Drainage swale

Everything You Need:

Tools: Garden stakes, shovel, hand tamper,

Materials: Fresh soil, 6 mil polyethylene sheeting, landscape fabric, course gravel, perforated drain pipe, splash block.

Standing water damages masonry, particularly if large quantities of water are allowed to permeate the base. Soil drainage is the key to preventing damage. In large low-lying areas, you can improve drainage by creating a shallow ditch, called a drainage swale, to carry runoff away from masonry. In some cases, more modest remedies, such as filler soil (below left) and rolled polyethylene (below right) are helpful.

Drainage Tips

Fill small low-lying areas by top-dressing them with soil. Spread the new soil evenly, then tamp it with a hand tamper and add soil as needed to fill the area.

A layer of polyethylene at the bottom of a site for a walk or driveway (pages 172 to 175) can protect the slab from the damaging effects of moisture.

How to Make a Drainage Swale

1 Use stakes to mark a route that will direct water toward a runoff area. The outlet must be lower than any point in the problem area. Remove the sod along the route and set it in the shade—you can re-lay it when the swale is completed.

2 Dig a 6"-deep trench, shaping the trench so it slopes gradually downward toward the outlet, and the sides and bottom are smooth.

3 Complete the swale by laying sod into the trench, then watering the area thoroughly to check the drainage.

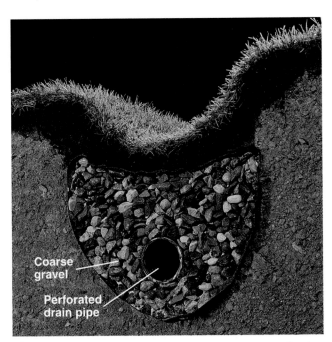

Coarse gravel

Perforated drain pipe

Splash block

OPTION: For severe drainage problems, dig a 1-ft.-deep swale angled slightly downward to the outlet point. Line the swale with landscape fabric. Spread a 2" layer of coarse gravel in the bottom of the swale, then lay perforated drain pipe over the gravel. Cover the pipe with a 5" layer of gravel, then wrap the landscape fabric over the top of the gravel. Cover the swale with soil and fresh sod (left). Set a splash block at the outlet to distribute the runoff and prevent erosion (right).

Mixing & Throwing Mortar

Watching a professional brick-layer at work is an impressive sight, even for do-it-yourselfers who have completed numerous masonry projects successfully. The mortar practically flies off the trowel and seems to end up in perfect position to accept the next brick or block.

Although "throwing mortar" is an acquired skill that takes years to perfect, you can use the basic techniques success-fully with just a little practice (pages 30 and 69).

The first critical element to handling mortar effectively is the mixture. If it's too thick, it will fall off the trowel in a heap, not in the smooth line that is your goal. Add too much water and the mortar becomes messy and weak. Follow the manufac-turer's directions, but keep in mind that the amount of water specified is an approximation. If you've never mixed mortar before, experiment with small amounts until you find a mixture that clings to the trowel just long enough for you to deliver a controlled, even line that holds its shape after settling. Note how much water you use in each batch, and record the best mixture.

Mix mortar for a large project in batches; on a hot, dry day a large batch will harden before you know it. If mortar begins to thicken, add water (called retempering); use retempered mortar within two hours.

Throwing mortar is a quick, smooth technique that requires practice. Load the trowel with mortar (page 30), then position the trowel a few inches above the starting point. In one motion, begin turning your wrist over and quickly move the trowel across the surface to spread mortar consistently. Proper mortar-throwing results in a rounded line about 2½" wide and about 2 ft. long.

Everything You Need:

Tools: Trowel, hoe, shovel.

Materials: Mortar mix, mortar box, plywood blocks.

Selecting the Right Mortar

Masonry mortar is a mixture of portland cement, sand, and water. Ingredients such as lime and gypsum are added to improve workability or control "setup" time. Every mortar mixture balances strength, workability, and other qualities. The strongest mortar is not always the best one for the job. A mortar that's too strong won't absorb stresses, such as those that occur as temperatures rise and fall. The result can be damage to masonry structures.

Each project and repair in this book includes a mortar mix recommendation. Always follow the guidelines for your project and the materials you've selected, and read the manufacturer's specifications on the mortar mix package. The chart below indicates the typical uses for the most commonly sold mortar mixes. Type N mortar mix is called for most often, because it offers a good blend of strength and workability.

Types of Mortar & Their Uses

Gone are the days when do-it-yourselfers had to mix mortar from scratch. These days, when you think of mortar, think of mortar mix, the standard term for the dry, prepackaged mixes available at home centers. For most of today's projects, simply select the proper mortar mixture, mix in water, and start to trowel. For some repair projects, adding a fortifier (page 241) may be recommended. You can also tint your mortar to match your other materials.

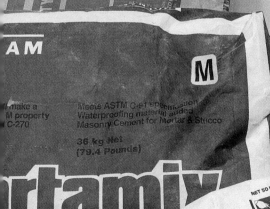

Type N
Medium-strength mortar for above grade outdoor use in non-load-bearing (freestanding) walls, barbecues, chimneys, soft stone masonry, and tuck-pointing.

Type S
High-strength mortar for exterior use at or below grade. Generally used in foundations, brick and block retaining walls, driveways, walks, and patios.

Type M
Very high-strength specialty mortar for load-bearing exterior stone walls, including stone retaining walls, and veneer applications.

Refractory Mortar
A calcium aluminate mortar that does not break down with exposure to high temperatures; used for mortaring around firebrick in fireplaces and barbecues. Chemical-set mortar is best, because it will cure even in wet conditions.

Glass Block Mortar
A specialty white type S mortar for glass block projects. Standard grey type S mortar is also acceptable for glass block projects.

How to Mix & Throw Mortar

1 Empty mortar mix into a mortar box and form a depression in the center. Add about ¾ of the recommended amount of water into the depression, then mix it in with a masonry hoe. Do not overwork the mortar. Continue adding small amounts of water and mixing until the mortar reaches the proper consistency. Do not mix too much mortar at one time—mortar is much easier to work with when it is fresh.

2 Set a piece of plywood on blocks at a convenient height, and place a shovelful of mortar onto the surface. Slice off a strip of mortar from the pile, using the edge of your mason's trowel. Slip the trowel point-first under the section of mortar and lift up.

3 Snap the trowel gently downward to dislodge excess mortar clinging to the edges. Position the trowel at the starting point, and "throw" a line of mortar onto the building surface (see technique photos, page 28). A good amount is enough to set three bricks. Do not get ahead of yourself. If you throw too much mortar, it will set before you are ready.

4 "Furrow" the mortar line by dragging the point of the trowel through the center of the mortar line in a slight back-and-forth motion. Furrowing helps distribute the mortar evenly.

Tips for Using Mortar with Stone

Mortar-set stone projects require more mortar than similar projects using brick or block because stones have highly irregular surfaces. Butter the mating surfaces of stones generously to fill in the peaks and valleys in each stone's surface.

Practice "buttering" stones so that each buttered surface fills the gap between one stone and the next. If the mating (adjoining) surfaces are highly contoured, butter both surfaces. You can also use the trowel to create a mound (above) or a depression to conform to the shape of the adjacent stone.

Tips for Special Mortar Treatments

Adding tint to mortar works best if you add the same amount to each batch throughout the project. Once you settle on a recipe, record it so you can mix the same proportions each time.

Use a stiff (dry) mix of mortar for tuck-pointing—it's less likely to shrink and crack. Start by mixing type N mortar mix with half the recommended water. Let the mixture stand for one hour, then add the remaining water and finish mixing.

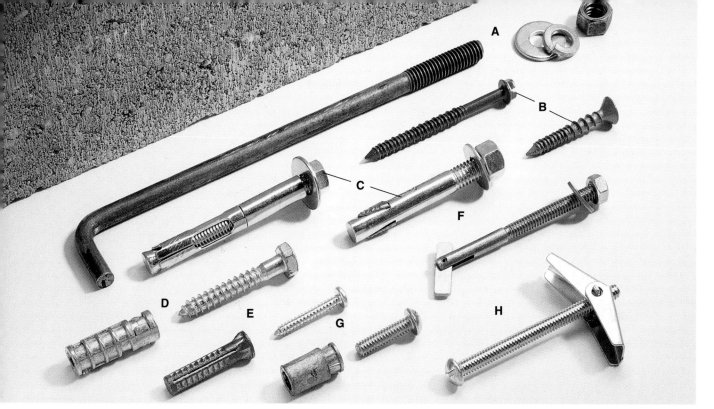

Masonry fasteners include: J-bolt with nut and washers (A) for setting railings on fresh concrete; self-tapping coated steel screws (B) for hanging lightweight hardware on vertical surfaces; sleeve anchor (left) and wedge anchor (right) (C) for mounting gates and other heavy objects on vertical surfaces; lag screw expansion shield and screw (D) for mounting gates and other heavy objects; plastic anchor and wood screw (E) for light-duty mounting; removable T-anchor (F) for small diameter holes; expansion shield "flush anchor" and screw (G) for applications where the top of the fastener must be flush with the masonry surface; spring-loaded toggle bolt (H) for mounting in the void of a brick or block.

Working with Masonry Fasteners

Masonry fasteners allow you to mount objects—from signs to gates—on masonry surfaces. The simplest and most effective method is to place the mounting hardware in fresh concrete or mortar (right) while it's still wet. Once the concrete or mortar sets, the hardware is secure and will remain firmly in place. Often, however, the decision to hang a sign, address plate, or gate comes long after the surface has hardened. The solution is to drill a hole with a masonry bit or hole saw, or—for a large post—chip out a hole with a maul and chisel. On horizontal surfaces, fill the hole with anchoring cement and place a J-bolt or other fastener in the cement. Hold or brace the fastener in place for several minutes until the cement begins to harden. On vertical surfaces, use metal fasteners rated to the weight of the object you are hanging.

Hardware installed in fresh mortar has the most durable hold, as well as a natural seal against moisture. Installing hardware on cured walls and pillars can also be effective, provided it's mounted with an approved fastener and sealed with masonry caulk to keep out moisture.

Tips for Setting Hardware in Concrete

Mount hardware in concrete when the concrete is still wet, for best results. When attaching a handrail to a freshly poured stoop, use hardware that attaches to a J-bolt. Embed the bolt so ¾" to 1" of it is exposed. Check for plumb and brace it in place for several minutes until the concrete becomes firm. Let the concrete cure for 24 hours before attaching the railing.

Reset loose masonry anchors by removing the anchors, filling the old holes with anchoring cement (anchoring cement expands as it dries, creating a tighter repair), then pressing new anchors into the fresh cement. Make sure the anchors are not disturbed while the cement sets up, usually about one hour.

Tips for Setting Hardware in Mortared Walls

Mount fasteners in fresh mortar for best results with brick, block, or stone structures. Sketch fastener locations on paper, so you can set the fasteners in the bed joints as you build. Check the alignment, then lay the next course. If you're installing hardware on an existing structure, mark locations for fasteners, then use a hammer drill with a carbide-tipped masonry bit to drill holes. Let the mortar cure for one week before installing gates or other heavy hardware.

Mount fasteners on masonry veneer, using a T-anchor or spring-loaded toggle bolt (page 32). Mark locations for the hardware, then drill holes according to the fastener specifications, using a hammer drill and a carbide-tipped masonry bit. Once fasteners are in place, seal around them with masonry caulk. Let the mortar cure for one week before installing gates or other heavy hardware.

Poured concrete can be shaped and finished to create a wide variety of surfaces and structures around your home. In the photo above, the steps and the walkway blend together gracefully. The poured-concrete construction creates the impression that the two elements are a single unit.

Working with Concrete

Poured concrete is one of the most versatile and durable building materials available. You can use it to make just about any type of outdoor structure. Concrete costs less than other building materials, such as pressure-treated lumber or brick pavers. With a decorative finish such as exposed aggregate, or a tint added to the wet mixture, you can vary concrete's appearance. Using simple tools, you can finish concrete to simulate brick pavers or flagstones (page 110), or use it to craft stepping stones with a personality all their own (pages 118 to 119).

Whether you're fashioning stepping stones or pouring a driveway, timing and preparation are the most important factors in working with concrete. Poured concrete yields the most durable

and attractive final finish when it is poured at an air temperature between 50° and 80°F and when the finishing steps are completed carefully in the order described in this section.

Yet, concrete will harden to its final form whether you have finished working it or not. The best insurance policy against running out of time is thorough site preparation. Good preparation means fewer delays at critical moments, and leaves you free to focus on placing and smoothing the concrete—not on staking down loose forms or locating misplaced tools.

Stick to smaller-scale projects until you're comfortable working with concrete, and recruit helpers if you're taking on a large project.

Common Concrete Projects

A concrete walkway in a backyard or at a garage or side entrance is a good starter project. The techniques, even for angled walkways like the one shown above, are basic. Because no frost footing is required in most cases, and because walkways can be built to follow gradual slopes, little site preparation is needed. See "Pouring a Concrete Walkway" (pages 106 to 109).

A patio can be built and finished to blend well with the surrounding elements of just about any yard and house. Using permanent forms between sections allows the entire project to be treated as a series of smaller projects. See "Building an Exposed-aggregate Patio" (pages 154 to 157).

Concrete steps are long-lasting structures that resist wear and tear. When finished with a non-skid surface, such as the broomed surface above, concrete steps offer a reliable walking surface. See Building Concrete Steps (pages 130 to 135).

A poured concrete footing creates a sturdy base for poured concrete projects, as well as for projects built from brick or block. Requirements for footings are defined in your local Building Code. See Pouring Footings (pages 56 to 59).

Good site preparation is one of the keys to a successful project. Patience and attention to detail when excavating, building forms, and establishing a subbase help ensure that your finished project is level and stable and will last for many years.

Preparing the Project Site

The basic steps in preparing a project site are:

1) Laying out the project, using stakes and strings;

2) Clearing the project area and removing sod;

3) Excavating the site to allow for a subbase and footings (as needed) and concrete;

4) Laying a subbase for drainage and stability and pouring footings (as needed);

5) Building and installing reinforced wood forms.

Proper site preparation varies from project to project and site to site. Plan on a subbase of compactible gravel. Some projects require footings (pages 56 to 59) that extend past the frost line, while others, such as sidewalks, do not. Ask your local building inspector if you need metal reinforcement.

If your yard slopes more than 1" per ft., you may need to add or remove soil to level the surface; a landscape engineer or a building inspector can advise you on how to prepare your yard for your project.

SAFETY TIP: Beware of buried electric and gas lines when digging. Contact your local public utility company before you start digging.

Everything You Need:

Tools: Rope, carpenter's square, hand maul, tape measure, mason's string, line level, spade, sod cutter, straightedge, level, wheelbarrow, shovel, hand tamper, circular saw, drill.

Materials: 2 × 4 lumber, 3" screws, compactible gravel, vegetable oil or commercial release agent.

Tips for Preparing the Project Site

Measure the slope of the building site to determine if you need to do grading work before you start your project. First, drive stakes at each end of the project area. Attach a mason's string between the stakes and use a line level to set it at level. At each stake, measure from the string to the ground. The difference between the measurements (in inches) divided by the distance between stakes (in feet) will give you the slope (in inches per foot). If the slope is greater than 1" per foot, you may need to regrade the site.

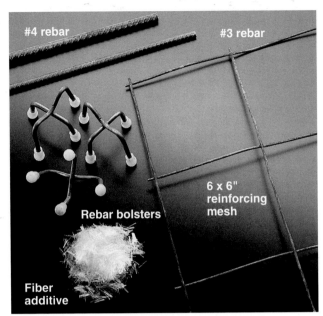

Reinforcement materials: *Metal rebar,* available in sizes ranging from #2 (1/8" diameter) to #5 (5/8" diameter) is used to reinforce narrow concrete slabs, like sidewalks, and in masonry walls. For most projects, #3 rebar (3/8" diameter) is suitable. *Wire mesh* (sometimes called re-mesh) is most common in 6 × 6" grids. It is usually used for broad surfaces, like patios. *Bolsters* suspend rebar and wire mesh off the subbase. *Fiber additive* is mixed into concrete to strengthen small projects that receive little traffic.

Add a compactible gravel subbase to provide a level, stable foundation for the concrete. The compactible gravel also improves drainage—an important consideration if you are building on soil that is high in clay content. For most building projects, pour a layer of compactible gravel about 5" thick, and use a tamper to compress it to 4".

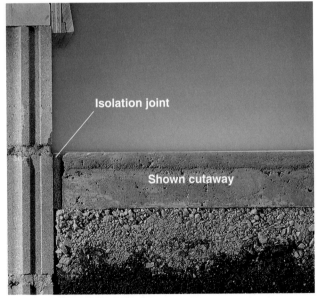

When pouring concrete next to structures, glue a 1/2"-thick piece of asphalt-impregnated fiber board to the adjoining structure to keep the concrete from bonding with the structure. The board creates an isolation joint, allowing the structures to move independently, minimizing the risk of damage.

How to Lay Out & Excavate a Building Site

1 Lay out a rough project outline with a rope or hose. Use a carpenter's square to set perpendicular lines. To create the actual layout, begin by driving wood stakes near each corner of the rough layout. The goal is to arrange the stakes so they are outside the actual project area, but in alignment with the borders of the project. Where possible, use two stakes set back 1 ft. from each corner, so strings intersect to mark each corner (below). NOTE: In projects built next to permanent structures, the structure will define one project side.

2 Connect the stakes with mason's strings. The strings should follow the actual project outlines. To make sure the strings are square, use the 3-4-5 triangle method (pages 178 to 179): measure and mark points 3 ft. out from one corner along one string, and 4 ft. out along the intersecting string at the corner. Measure between the points, and adjust the positions of the strings until the distance between the points is exactly 5 ft. A helper will make this easier.

3 Reset the stakes, if necessary, to conform to the positions of the squared strings. Check all corners with the 3-4-5 method, and adjust until the entire project area is exactly square. This can be a lengthy process with plenty of trial and error, but it is very important to the success of the project, especially if you plan to build on the concrete surface.

Line level

4 Attach a line level to one of the mason's strings to use as a reference. Adjust the string up or down as necessary until it is level. Adjust the other strings until they are level, making sure that intersecting strings contact one another (this ensures that they are all at the same height relative to ground level).

5 Most concrete surfaces should have a slight slope to direct water runoff, especially if they are near your house. To create a slope, shift the level mason's strings on opposite sides of the project downward on their stakes (the lower end should be farther away from the house). To create a standard slope of ⅛" per foot, multiply the distance between the stakes on one side (in feet) by ⅛. For example, if the stakes were 10 ft. apart, the result would be ¹⁰⁄₈ (1¼"). You would move the strings down 1¼" on the stakes on the low ends.

6 Start excavating by removing the sod. Use a sod cutter if you wish to reuse the sod elsewhere in your yard (lay the sod as soon as possible). Otherwise, use a square-end spade to cut away sod. Strip off the sod at least 6" beyond the mason's strings to make room for 2 × 4 forms. You may need to remove the strings temporarily for this step.

7 Make a story pole as a guide for excavating the site. First, measure down to ground level from the high end of a slope line. Add 7½" to that distance (4" for the subbase material and 3½" for the concrete if you are using 2 × 4 forms). Mark the total distance on the story pole, measuring from one end. Remove soil from the site with a spade. Use the story pole to make sure the bottom of the site is consistent (the same distance from the slope line at all points) as you dig. Check points at the center of the site using a straightedge and a level placed on top of the soil.

8 Lay a subbase for the project (unless your project requires a frost footing, pages 56 to 59). Pour a 5"-thick layer of compactible gravel in the project site, and tamp until the gravel is even and compressed to 4" in depth. NOTE: The subbase should extend at least 6" beyond the project outline.

How to Build & Install Wood Forms

1 A form is a frame, usually made from 2 × 4 lumber, laid around a project site to contain poured concrete and establish its thickness. Cut 2 × 4s to create a frame with inside dimensions equal to the total size of the project.

2 Use the mason's strings that outline the project (pages 38 to 39) as a reference for setting form boards in place. Starting with the longest form board, position the boards so the inside edges are directly below the strings.

3 Cut several pieces of 2 × 4 at least 12" long to use as stakes. Trim one end of each stake to a sharp point. Drive the stakes at 3-ft. intervals at the outside edges of the form boards, positioned to support any joints in the form boards.

4 Drive 3" deck screws through the stakes and into the form board one one side. Set a level so it spans the staked side of the form and the opposite form board, and use the level as a guide as you stake the second form board so it is level with the first (for large projects, use the mason's strings as the primary guide for setting the height of all form boards).

5 Once the forms are staked and leveled, drive 3" deck screws at the corners. Coat the insides of the forms with vegetable oil or a commercial release agent so concrete won't bond with them. Tip: Tack nails to the outsides of the forms to mark locations for control joints at intervals roughly 1½ times the slab's width (but no more than 30 times its thickness).

Variations for Building Forms

Use plywood (top left photo) for building taller forms for projects like concrete steps (pages 130 to 135). Gang-cut plywood form sides, and brace with 2 × 4 arms attached to stakes and 2 × 4 cleats at the sides.
Use the earth as a form (bottom left photo) when building footings for poured concrete building projects (page 57). Use standard wood forms for the tops of footings for building with brick or block, when the footing will be visible. Create curves (above, right) with ⅛" hardboard attached at the inside corners of a form frame. Drive support stakes behind the curved form.

Tips for Laying Metal Reinforcement

Cut metal rebar with a reciprocating saw that is equipped with a metal-cutting blade (cutting metal rebar with a hacksaw can take 5 to 10 minutes per cut). Use bolt cutters to cut wire mesh.

Overlap joints in metal rebar by at least 12", then bind the ends together with heavy-gauge wire. Overlap seams in wire mesh reinforcement by 12".

Leave at least 1" of clearance between the forms and the edges or ends of metal reinforcement. Use bolsters or small chunks of concrete to raise wire mesh reinforcement off the subbase, but make sure it is at least 2" below the tops of the forms.

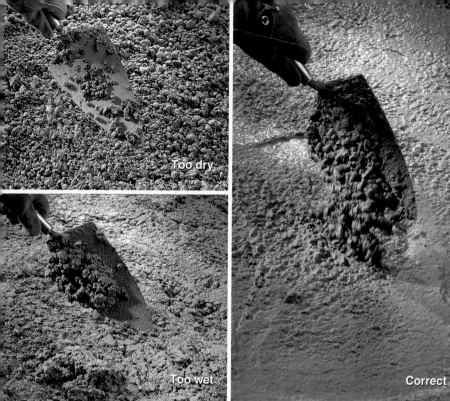

Too dry

Too wet

Correct

Estimating & Mixing Concrete

If you are mixing concrete on-site, you can purchase the ingredients separately and blend them or purchase bags of pre-mixed concrete, and simply add water. For small do-it-yourself projects, premixed products are recommended. By following the instructions on the bag, you can achieve uniform results from one batch to the next. Never mix less than a full bag of mix, however, since key ingredients may have settled to the bottom.

For smaller projects, a wheelbarrow or mortar box makes a good mixing container. For larger projects, consider renting or buying a power mixer, or having the concrete delivered by a ready-mix company.

A good mixture is crucial to any successful concrete project. Properly mixed concrete is damp enough to form in your hand when you squeeze, and dry enough to hold its shape. If the mixture is too dry, the aggregate will be difficult to work, and will not smooth out easily to produce an even, finished appearance. A wet mixture will slide off the trowel, and may cause cracking and other defects in the finished surface.

Components of Concrete

The basic ingredients of concrete are the same, whether the concrete is mixed from scratch, purchased premixed, or delivered by a ready-mix company. Portland cement is the bonding agent. It contains crushed lime, cement, and other bonding minerals. Sand and a combination of aggregates add volume and strength to the mix. Water activates the cement, then evaporates, allowing the concrete to dry into a solid mass. By varying the ratios of the ingredients, professionals can create concrete with special properties that are suited for specific situations.

Premixed concrete products contain all the components of concrete. Just add water, mix, and pour. Usually sold in 60-lb. bags that yield roughly ½ cu. ft., these products include ingredients with specific properties for specific applications. General-purpose concrete mix (A) is usually the least expensive, and is suitable for most do-it-yourself, poured concrete projects. Fiber-reinforced concrete mix (B) contains strands of fiberglass that increase the strength of the concrete. If approved by your local building inspector, you can use fiber-reinforced concrete for some slabs, instead of general-purpose concrete, eliminating the need for metal reinforcement. High-early-strength premixed concrete (C) contains agents that cause it to set quickly—a desirable property if you are pouring in cool weather. Sand mix (D) contains no mixed aggregate, and is used only for surface repairs where larger aggregate is not desirable.

Tips for Estimating Concrete

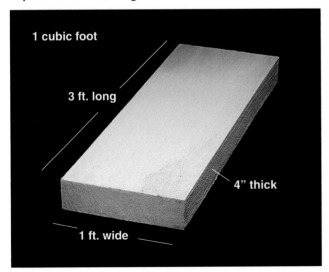

Concrete Coverage		
Volume	Thickness	Surface Coverage
1 cu. yd.	2"	160 sq. ft.
1 cu. yd.	3"	110 sq. ft.
1 cu. yd.	4"	80 sq. ft
1 cu. yd.	5"	65 sq. ft.
1 cu. yd.	6"	55 sq. ft.
1 cu. yd.	8"	40 sq. ft.

Measure the width and length of the project in feet, then multiply the dimensions to get the square footage. Measure the thickness in feet (4" thick equals ⅓ ft.), then multiply the square footage times the thickness to get the cubic footage. For example, 1 ft. × 3 ft. × ⅓ ft. = 1 cu. ft. Twenty-seven cubic feet equals one cubic yard.

Coverage rates for poured concrete are determined by the thickness of the slab. The same volume of concrete will yield less surface area if the thickness of the slab is increased. The chart above shows the relationship between slab thickness, surface area, and volume.

How to Mix Concrete by Hand

1 Empty premixed concrete bags into a mortar box or wheelbarrow. Form a hollow in the mound of dry mix, then pour water into the hollow. Start with one gallon of clean tap water per 60-lb. bag.

2 Work with a hoe, continuing to add water until a good consistency is achieved (page 42). Clear out any dry pockets from the corners. Do not over-work the mix. Also, keep track of how much water you use in the first batch so you will have a reliable recipe for subsequent batches.

How to Mix Concrete with a Power Mixer

1 Fill a bucket with 1 gallon of water for each 60-lb. bag of concrete you will use in the batch (for most power mixers, 3 bags is workable). Pour in half the water. Before you start power-mixing, review the op-erating instructions carefully.

2 Add all of the dry ingredients, then mix for one minute. Pour in water as needed until the proper consistency is achieved (page 42), and mix for three minutes. Pivot the mixing drum to empty the concrete into a wheelbarrow. Rinse out the drum immediately.

Have ready-mix concrete delivered for large projects. Prepare the site and build the forms, and try to have helpers on hand to help you place and tool the concrete when it arrives.

Ordering Ready-mix Concrete

For large concrete jobs (1 cubic yard or more), have ready-mix concrete delivered to your site. Although it is more expensive, it saves time. Seek referrals, and check your telephone directory under "Concrete" for ready-mix sources.

Tips for preparing for concrete delivery:

• Fully prepare the building site (pages 36 to 41).

• Discuss your project with the experts at the ready-mix company. They will help you decide how much and what type of concrete you need. To help you determine your quantity needs, see the chart on page 43.

• Call the supplier the day before the scheduled pour to confirm the quantity and delivery time.

• Read the receipt you get from the driver. It will tell you at what time the concrete was mixed. Before you accept the concrete, make sure no more than 90 minutes has elapsed between the time it was mixed and the time it was delivered.

Prepare a clear delivery path to the project site, so when the truck rolls up you are ready to pour. Lay planks over the forms and subbase to make a roadway for the wheelbarrows or concrete hoppers. If you have an asphalt or concrete driveway that is cracking, have the truck park on the street to prevent further damage.

Placing Concrete

Placing concrete involves pouring it into forms, then leveling and smoothing it with special masonry tools. Once the surface is smooth and level, control joints (step 5, page 40 and pages 48 to 49) are cut and the edges are rounded. Special attention to detail in these steps will result in a professional appearance. NOTE: If you plan to add a special finish, read "Finishing & Curing Concrete" (pages 52 to 53) before you begin your project.

Everything You Need:

Tools: Wheelbarrow, hoe, spade, hammer, mason's trowel, float, groover, edger.

Materials: Concrete, 2 × 4 lumber, mixing container, water container.

Start pouring concrete at the farthest point from the concrete source, and work your way back.

Tips for Pouring Concrete

Do not overload your wheelbarrow. Experiment with sand or dry mix to find a comfortable, controllable volume. This also helps you get a feel for how many wheelbarrow loads it will take to complete your project.

Lay planks over the forms to make a ramp for the wheelbarrow. Avoid disturbing the building site by using ramp supports. Make sure you have a flat, stable surface between the concrete source and the forms.

How to Place Concrete

1 Load the wheelbarrow with fresh concrete. Make sure you have a clear path from the source to the site. Always load wheelbarrows from the front; loading wheelbarrows from the side can cause tipping.

2 Pour concrete in evenly spaced loads (each load is called a "pod"). Start at the end farthest from the concrete source, and pour so the top of the pod is a few inches above the top of the forms. Do not pour too close to the forms. NOTE: If you are using a ramp, stay clear of the end of the ramp.

3 Continue to place concrete pods next to preceding pods, working away from the first pod. Do not pour more concrete than you can tool at one time. Keep an eye on the concrete to make sure it does not harden before you can start tooling.

4 Distribute concrete evenly in the project area, using a masonry hoe. Work the concrete with a hoe until it is fairly flat, and the surface is slightly above the top of the forms. Remove excess concrete with a shovel.

(continued next page)

How to Place Concrete (continued)

5 Immediately work the blade of a spade between the inside edges of the form and the concrete to remove trapped air bubbles that can weaken the concrete.

6 Rap the forms with a hammer or the blade of the shovel to help settle the concrete. This also draws finer aggregates in the concrete against the forms, creating a smoother surface on the sides. This is especially important when building steps.

7 Use a screed board—a straight piece of 2 × 4 long enough to rest on opposite forms—to remove the excess concrete before bleed water appears. Move the screed board in a sawing motion from left to right, and keep the screed flat as you work. If screeding leaves any valleys in the surface, add fresh concrete in the low areas and screed to level.

8 Cut control joints at marked locations (step 5, page 40) with a mason's trowel, using a straight 2 × 4 as a guide. Control joints are designed to control where the slab cracks in the future, as natural heaving and settling occur. Without control joints, a slab may develop a jagged, disfiguring crack.

9 Wait until bleed water disappears (see box), then float in an arcing motion, with the leading edge of the tool up. Stop floating as soon as the surface is smooth.

Understanding Bleed Water

Timing is key to an attractive concrete finish. When concrete is poured, the heavy materials gradually sink, leaving a thin layer of water—known as *bleed water*—on the surface. To achieve an attractive finish, it's important to let bleed water dry before proceeding with other steps. Follow these rules to avoid problems:

• Settle and screed the concrete and add control joints (steps 5 through 8) immediately after pouring and before bleed water appears. Otherwise, crazing, spalling, and other flaws (page 243) are likely.

• Let bleed water dry before floating or edging. Concrete should be hard enough that foot pressure leaves no more than a ¼"-deep impression.

• Do not overfloat the concrete; it may cause bleed water to reappear. Stop floating (step 9) if a sheen appears, and resume when it is gone.

NOTE: Bleed water does not appear with air-entrained concrete, which is used in regions where temperatures often fall below freezing.

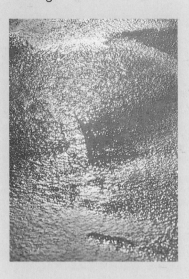

10 Once any bleed water has dried, draw a groover across the precut control joints (step 8), using a straight 2 × 4 as a guide. You may need to make several passes to create a smooth control joint.

11 Shape concrete with an edging tool between the forms and the concrete to create a smooth, finished appearance. You may need to make several passes. Use a wood float to smooth out any marks left by the groover or edger.

Building with Concrete: A Step-by-Step Overview

The project shown on these pages provides a basic overview of the techniques and processes used in building with concrete. The project features the pouring of a simple concrete slab that will serve as a base for a decorative-block screen (see pages 182 to 183 for construction of the screen). Refer to the cited pages for more information on the steps shown.

Because the project shown serves as a base for concrete block, dry-lay the block on the project site to determine the size of the slab (page 182).

1 Create a plan for the project (pages 12 to 15 and 42 to 43), then use stakes and mason's strings to outline the project. In the photo above, the 3-4-5 method of squaring up a layout is being used (step 2, page 38). After the layout is established, remove sod and excavate soil in the project site (step 6, page 39).

2 Create a subbase for the project by tamping compactible gravel to a consistent depth. Use a story pole to guide your work (step 7, page 39).

3 Install 2 × 4 forms around the project site (pages 40 to 41). Attach isolation boards to any permanent structures that will adjoin the project (page 37). Install any reinforcement required for the project (page 41). NOTE: If your project requires footings, pour them before preparing the subbase.

4 Calculate the volume of concrete needed for the job (see chart, page 43), and mix the concrete or have it delivered to the work site. Place the concrete into the forms, then use a masonry hoe to distribute it evenly. Work around the inside edges of the forms with a shovel and rap the forms with a hammer to release air bubbles and settle the concrete (step 6, page 48).

5 Level off the concrete so it is even with the tops of the forms, using a screed board. Let any bleed water dry (page 49), then smooth the surface with a float. If you plan to add a decorative finish, such as exposed aggregate (pages 52 to 53), do that before finishing the concrete.

6 Form control joints, using a mason's trowel and groover (step 8, page 48 and step 10, page 49), then shape the edges of the concrete at the forms, using an edger. Cover the concrete with plastic and let it cure for a week.

7 Remove the plastic and the forms, then backfill up to the edges of the concrete with dirt. Apply concrete sealer to protect the concrete during seasonal freeze-thaw cycles (pages 54 to 55).

Exposed aggregate. Sometimes called "seeding," applying decorative aggregate to a fresh concrete surface creates an attractive effect with many design options. The photo above shows what various aggregates look like when they are used for an exposed-aggregate surface.

Broomed finish. Tool the concrete, then drag a broom across it. Wait until concrete is firm to the touch to achieve a finer texture and a more weather-resistant surface.

Finishing & Curing Concrete

Finishing and curing are critical final steps in a concrete project. They ensure that concrete reaches its maximum strength and remains free of defects that harm its appearance. There are many theories on the best way to cure concrete. In general, a good rule is to keep concrete damp and covered with plastic for at least a week.

A decorative finish dresses up concrete's appearance. Exposed-aggregate finishes (page 53) are common on walkways and patios. Brooming (above) is a good option for improved traction. Stamping patterns (pages 110 to 111) is a popular way to create surfaces that imitate brick and other materials. Look around your neighborhood for other examples of creative finishes.

Everything You Need:

Tools: Broom, wheelbarrow, shovel, magnesium float, groover, edger, hose, coarse brush.

Materials: Plastic sheeting, "seeding" aggregate, water.

How to Cure Concrete

Keep concrete covered and damp for at least a week to maximize strength and to minimize surface defects. Lift the plastic occasionally and wet the surface so the concrete cures slowly.

How to Create an Exposed-aggregate Finish

1 After smoothing the surface with a screed board (step 7, page 48), let any bleed water disappear (page 49), then spread clean, washed aggregate evenly with a shovel or by hand. Spread smaller aggregate (up to 1" in diameter) in a single layer; for larger aggregate, maintain a separation between stones that is roughly equal to the size of one stone.

2 Pat the aggregate down with the screed board, then float the surface with a magnesium float until a thin layer of concrete covers the stones. Do not overfloat. If bleed water appears, stop floating and let it dry before completing the step (page 49). If you are seeding a large area, cover it with plastic to keep the concrete from hardening too quickly.

3 Cut control joints and tool the edges (step 8, page 48 and steps 10-11, page 49). Let concrete set for 30 to 60 minutes, then mist a section of the surface and scrub with a brush to remove the concrete covering the aggregate. If brushing dislodges some of the stones, reset them and try again later. When you can scrub without dislodging stones, mist and scrub the entire surface to expose the aggregate. Rinse clean. Do not let the concrete dry too long, or it will be difficult to scrub off.

4 After the concrete has cured for one week (page 52), remove the covering and rinse the surface with a hose. If a residue remains, try scrubbing it clean. If scrubbing is ineffective, wash the surface with a muriatic acid solution, then rinse immediately and thoroughly with water. OPTION: After three weeks, apply exposed-aggregate sealer (page 55).

Sealing & Maintaining Concrete

Concrete lasts longer if it is protected with a clear concrete sealer so that water does not permeate the surface. In addition to sealer, there are other special-purpose products designed for concrete surfaces. Specially formulated concrete paints, for example, help keep minerals in the concrete from leeching through paint and hardening into a white, dusty film called *efflorescence*.

Regular cleaning, an important element of concrete maintenance, prevents deterioration from oils and deicing salts. Use concrete cleaning products for scheduled cleanings, and special solutions (page 255) for specific types of stains. Concrete sealer should be reapplied annually in harsh conditions.

Use waterproof concrete paint on concrete surfaces. Concrete paint is formulated to resist chalking and efflorescence. It is sold in several stock colors, or you can have custom colors mixed from a tint base.

> ### Everything You Need:
>
> Tools: Paint brush, paint roller and tray, dust brush and pan, caulk gun, paint pad.
>
> Materials: Masonry paint, paint thinner, repair caulk, sealer, concrete recoating product.

Tips for Cleaning & Maintaining Concrete

Clean oil stains by dampening sawdust with paint thinner, then applying the sawdust over the stain. The paint thinner will break apart the stain, allowing the oil to be absorbed by the sawdust. Wipe up with a broom when finished, and reapply as necessary.

Fill control joints in sidewalks, driveways and other concrete surfaces with concrete repair caulk. The caulk fills the joint, preventing water from accumulating and causing damage to the concrete.

Options for Sealing Concrete

Exposed-aggregate sealer is specially formulated to keep aggregate from loosening. It should be applied about three weeks after the concrete surface is poured. To apply, wash the surface thoroughly and allow it to dry. Pour some sealer into a roller tray. Make a puddle of sealer in a corner and spread it out evenly with a paint roller and extension pole.

Clear concrete sealer helps create a water-resistant seal on the surface of new or old concrete. Popular concrete sealing products today are acrylic based and do not attract dirt. Most manufacturer's recommend keeping fresh concrete damp and covered with plastic for at least a week before applying sealer. Read the manufacturer's instructions carefully before applying sealer.

Masonry recoating products are applied like paint, but they look like fresh concrete when they dry. They are used frequently to improve the appearance of walls, although they generally have little value as waterproofing agents.

Footings are required by Building Code for concrete, stone, brick, and block structures that adjoin other permanent structures or that exceed the height specified by local codes. *Frost footings* extend 8" to 12" below the frost line. *Slab footings*, which are typically 8" thick, may be recommended for low, freestanding structures built using mortar or poured concrete. Before starting your project, ask a building inspector about footing recommendations and requirements for your area.

Pouring Footings

Footings provide a stable, level base for brick, block, stone, and poured concrete structures. They distribute the weight of the structure evenly, prevent sinking, and keep structures from moving during seasonal freeze-thaw cycles.

The required depth of a footing is usually determined by the *frost line*, which varies by region. The frost line is the point nearest ground level where the soil does not freeze. In colder climates, it is likely to be 48" or deeper. Frost footings (footings designed to keep structures from moving during freezing temperatures) should extend 12" below the frost line for the area. Your local building inspector can tell you the frost line depth for your area.

Tips for Planning:

• Describe the proposed structure to your local building inspector to find out whether it requires a footing, and whether the footing needs reinforcement. In some cases, 8"-thick slab footings can be used, as long as the subbase provides plenty of drainage.

• Keep footings separate from adjoining structures by installing an isolation board (page 37).

• For smaller poured concrete projects, consider pouring the footing and the structure as one unit.

• A multi-wall project such as a barbecue may require a floating footing (page 235).

Options for Forming Footings

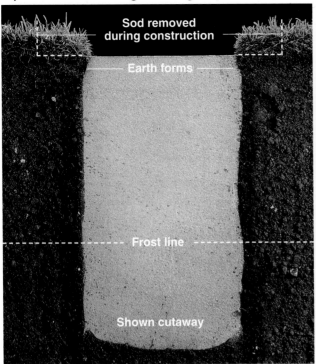

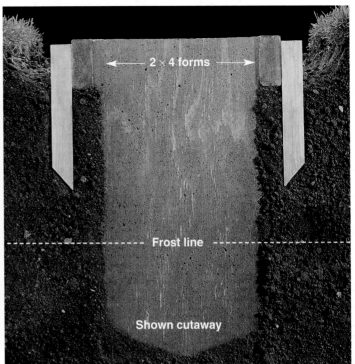

For poured concrete, use the earth as a form. Strip sod from around the project area, then strike off the concrete with a screed board resting on the earth at the edges of the top of the trench.

For brick, block, and stone, build level, recessed wood forms. Rest the screed board on the frames when you strike off the concrete to create a flat, even surface for stacking masonry units.

Tips for Building Footings

Make footings twice as wide as the wall or structure they will support. They also should extend at least 12" past the ends of the project area.

Add tie-rods if you will be pouring concrete over the footing. After the concrete sets up, press 12" sections of rebar 6" into the concrete. The tie-rods will anchor the footing to the structure it supports.

How to Pour a Footing

1 Make a rough outline of the footing, using a rope or hose. Outline the project area with stakes and mason's string (page 38).

2 Strip away sod 6" outside the project area on all sides, then excavate the trench for the footing to a depth 12" below the frost line.

3 Build and install a 2 × 4 form frame for the footing, aligning it with the mason's strings (page 40). Stake the form in place, and adjust to level.

VARIATION: If your project abuts another structure, such as a house foundation, slip a piece of fiber board into the trench to create an isolation joint between the footing and the structure (page 37). Use a few dabs of construction adhesive to hold it in place.

4 Make two #3 rebar grids to reinforce the footing. For each grid, cut two pieces of #3 rebar 8" shorter than the length of the footing, and two pieces 4" shorter than the depth of the footing. Bind the pieces together with 16-gauge wire, forming a rectangle. Set the rebar grids upright in the trench, leaving 4" of space between the grids and the walls of the trench. Coat the inside edge of the form with vegetable oil or commerical release agent.

5 Mix and pour concrete, so it reaches the tops of the forms (pages 46 to 49). Screed the surface, using a 2 x 4. Add tie-rods if needed (page 57). Float the concrete until it is smooth and level.

6 Cure the concrete for one week before you build on the footing. Remove the forms and backfill around the edges of the footing (page 51).

Fast-setting concrete requires no mixing, making it ideal for pouring post footings. Just fill the post hole with the dry concrete mix, then add water. If you plan to work or shape the top of the footing, premix the concrete, but act quickly—some concrete blends will set in as little as 20 minutes.

Setting Posts in Concrete

Whether it's supporting a fence, a mailbox, or a basketball hoop, a post will stand solid and straight for many years if you anchor it in concrete. Concrete post footings are easy to pour, and they protect wood and metal posts from rusting and rotting.

For posts that support structures, such as a deck, most building codes require that the footings extend below the frost line (page 56 to 57). Check with your local building inspector for footing requirements for your project.

Everything You Need:

Tools: Shovel, clamshell digger, digging bar, hand tamper, saw, drill, maul, level, trowel.

Materials: Gravel, concrete mix, post lumber, 2 × 4 lumber, screws, wood sealer (for wood posts).

Tips for Setting Posts

To discourage rot, use cedar, redwood, or pressure-treated pine for wood posts. Seal cut ends with a wood sealer before setting the posts in concrete. Shape the tops of posts or attach post caps to prevent water from settling and promoting rot.

To brace metal posts, fashion a 2 × 4 collar. Assemble the collar around the middle of the post, using 3" deck screws. Use shims to hold the collar in place. Plumb the post, and attach braces to two adjacent sides of the collar (step 3, page 61).

How to Set a Post in Concrete

1 Dig a hole that is three times wider than the post width (or diameter) and as deep as ⅓ the post length, plus 6". Use a clamshell digger for most of the digging and a digging bar to dislodge rocks and loosen compacted soil.

2 Pour 6" of loose gravel into the bottom of the hole to ensure proper drainage. Tamp the gravel, using a hand tamper or wood post.

3 Set the post in the hole. Attach 2 × 4 braces to two adjacent faces of the post. Check for plumb, then drive a stake into the ground near the end of each brace, and attach the ends of the braces to the stakes.

4 Fill the hole 4" below ground level with fast-setting concrete. Check the post again to make sure it is plumb, then add the recommended amount of water. When it's dry, cover the footing with soil or sod.

OPTION: For added protection against rot, premix the concrete and overfill the hole slightly. Using a trowel, quickly shape the concrete to form a crown that will shed water away from the post.

Create a formal setting for your home with brick and block. The brick steps and brick veneer on the house above give the home a distinctive appearance. Brick has a significant advantage over other building materials: it is exceptionally easy to maintain.

Working with Brick & Block

Masonry professionals often speak of the satisfaction of working with brick and block. With each brick or block that's laid, they can see evidence of a project's progress, whether it's a concrete block garden wall (pages 180 to 181), a brick-paver patio (pages 146 to 153), or a veneer wall (pages 210 to 213).

When applied with good design principles, the colors and textures of brick and block can give your entire home or yard a sense of balanced composition. Brick and block building projects,

such as those shown on the next page, can also add practical features to your house and yard.

Careful planning and a thoughtful design will help you build a project that makes sense for your house, your yard, and your budget. Plan your project to avoid unnecessary cutting of masonry units (page 66).

Brick and decorative block colors and textures vary widely by region, reflecting regional trends. Product lines are often discontinued without notice, so buy extra materials for future repairs.

Common Brick & Block Projects

A garden wall is a good project for beginners. If the wall is under 3 ft. in height and is not tied to another structure, a frost footing may be unnecessary. Check with your local building inspector: You may be able to simplify the project by building on top of a slab footing. First, learn the basic techniques for building with brick (pages 64 to 71).

A decorative-block screen creates a visual barrier without completely blocking light. The open structure also allows full air circulation, making screens such as the one shown above excellent structures for accenting gardens and enclosing utility areas (pages 182 to 183).

A brick-paver step landing and planter are effective examples of combining projects to achieve results that are both attractive and useful. The paver landing was set into mortar directly over the existing sidewalk (pages 143 to 145 and 230 to 231).

Brick veneer usually is applied to houses during new construction as an attractive design element. But if your foundation walls are in good shape, you can install it as a retrofit project to update the appearance of your home (pages 210 to 213). If the foundation is questionable in any way, have a contractor examine it before you start your project.

Common types of brick and block used for residential construction include: decorative block (A) available colored or plain, decorative concrete pavers (B), fire brick (C), standard 8 × 8 × 16" concrete block (D), half block (E), combination corner block (F), queen-sized brick (G), standard brick pavers (H), standard building bricks (I), and limestone wall cap (J).

Building Techniques for Brick & Block

Start a patio, wall, or any other brick or block project by identifying a suitable construction method and practicing the techniques you'll use along the way. If you are building a wall (pages 72 to 75) or covering an old concrete slab with brick or brick pavers (pages 114 to 115), you'll need to use wet mortar to create a strong bond. The sand-set and dry mortar techniques are suitable for patios and driveways, where sand or dry mortar is enough to hold the bricks firmly in place. Most block walls are built with wet mortar, but an attractive garden wall is easily built by dry-laying blocks and coating them with surface bonding cement (pages 214 to 215).

In addition to settling on a construction method, you need to select a style (above) and pattern (page 65) to match your tastes and the construction method. Use the chart on page 17 to estimate how many bricks or blocks you'll need.

Interlocking brick pavers come in many shapes and colors. Two popular paver styles include UNI-Decor (left) and Symetry (right). (See page 281 for more information on these products.) Patios made with interlocking pavers may have a border row made from standard brick pavers.

Common Patterns for Standard Brick & Brick Pavers

Standard bricks and pavers can be arranged in several patterns, including: running bond (A) and jack-on-jack (B), a pattern which is called *stack bond* when used in brick projects. Stack bond is not as strong as running bond. Reinforcement is typically required when laying up bricks in this pattern. Pavers can also be arranged in a herringbone (C) or basket weave pattern (D). Jack-on-jack and basket weave require fewer cut pavers along the edges. Standard pavers have spacing lugs on the sides that automatically set the joints at ⅛" width.

Installation Variations for Brick Pavers

Sand-set: Pavers rest on a 1" bed of sand laid over a 4" compactible gravel subbase. Rigid plastic edging holds the sand base in place. Joints are ⅛" wide, and are packed with sand, which holds the pavers securely yet allows them to shift slightly as temperatures change.

Dry mortar: Installation is similar to sand-set, but joints are ⅜" wide, and are packed with a mixture of sand and mortar, soaked with water, and finished with a V-shaped mortar tool. Dry-mortar installation has a more finished masonry look than a sand-set one, but the joints must be repaired periodically.

Wet mortar: This method often is used when pavers are installed over an old concrete patio or sidewalk (pages 114 to 115). Joints are ½" wide. Wet mortar installation can also be used with flagstone. For edging on a wet mortar patio, use rigid plastic edging or paver bricks set on end.

Tips for Planning a Brick or Block Project

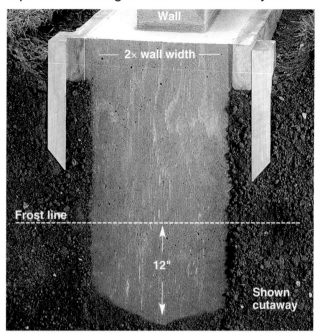

Build a frost footings if a structure is more than 2 ft. tall or if it is tied to another permanent structure (see photo, page opposite, bottom left). Frost footings should be twice as wide as the structure they support and should extend 8" to 12" below the frost line (pages 56 to 59).

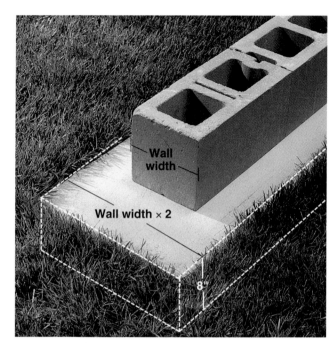

Pour a reinforced concrete slab for brick, block, stone, or poured concrete structures that are free-standing and under 2 ft. tall. The slab should be twice the wall's width, flush with ground level, and at least 8" thick. Ask your building inspector about local requirements. Slabs are poured using the techniques for pouring a walkway (pages 102 to 103, and 106 to 109).

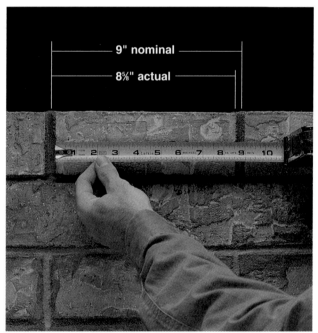

Do not add mortar joint thickness to total project dimensions when planning brick and block projects. The actual sizes of bricks and blocks are ⅜" smaller than the nominal size to allow for ⅜"-wide mortar joints. For example, a 9" (nominal) brick has an actual dimension of 8⅝", so a wall that is built with four 9" bricks and ⅜" mortar joints will have a finished length of 36" (4 × 9").

Test project layouts using ⅜" spacers between masonry units to make sure the planned dimensions work. If possible, create a plan that uses whole bricks or blocks, reducing the amount of cutting required.

Select a construction design that makes sense for your project. There are two basic methods used in stacking brick or block. Structures that are only one unit wide are called *single wythe,* and are typically used for projects like brick barbecues or planters, and for brick veneers. *Double-wythe* walls are two units wide and are used in free-standing applications. Most concrete-block structures are single wythe.

Build end-support pillars at the free ends of structures, especially when building with nonstructural block, such as the decorative block shown above. This support pillar uses 6 × 6" concrete blocks.

Keep structures as low as you can. Local codes require frost footings and additional reinforcement for permanent walls or structures that exceed maximum height restrictions. You can often simplify your project by designing walls that are below the maximum height.

Add a lattice panel or another decorative element to permanent walls to create greater privacy without having to add structural reinforcement to the masonry structure.

Tips for Reinforcing Brick & Block Structures

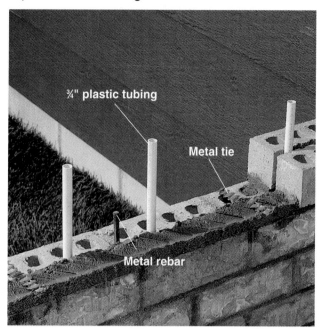

For double-wythe brick projects, use metal ties between wythes for reinforcement. Insert ties directly into the mortar 2 to 3 ft. apart, every third course. Insert metal rebar into the gap between wythes every 4 to 6 ft. (check local building codes). Insert ¾"-diameter plastic tubing between wythes to keep them aligned. Pour a thin mixture of mortar between the wythes to improve the strength of the wall.

For block projects, fill the empty spaces (cores) of the block with thin mortar. Insert sections of metal rebar into the mortar to increase vertical strength. Check with your local building inspector to determine reinforcement requirements, if any.

Provide horizontal reinforcement on brick or block walls by setting metal reinforcing strips into the mortar every third course. Metal reinforcing strips, along with most other reinforcing products, can be purchased from brick and block suppliers. Overlap the ends of metal strips 6" where they meet.

Tips for Working with Brick

Make practice runs on a 2 × 4 to help you perfect your mortar-throwing (pages 28 to 31) and bricklaying techniques. You can clean and reuse the bricks to make many practice runs if you find it helpful, but do not reuse the bricks in your actual project—old mortar can impede bonding.

Test the water absorption rate of bricks to determine their density. Squeeze out 20 drops of water in the same spot on the surface of a brick. If the surface is completely dry after 60 seconds, dampen the bricks with water before you lay them to prevent them from absorbing moisture from the mortar before it has a chance to set.

Use a T-square and pencil to mark several bricks for cutting. Make sure the ends of the bricks are all aligned.

Mark angled cuts by dry-laying the project (as shown with pavers above) and setting the brick or block in position. Allow for ⅜" joints in mortared projects. Pavers have spacing lugs that set the spacing at ⅛". Mark cutting lines with a pencil, using a straightedge where practical to mark straight lines.

How to Score & Cut Brick

Score all four sides of the brick first with a brickset chisel and maul when cuts fall over the web area, and not over the core. Tap the chisel to leave scored cutting marks ⅛" to ¼" deep, then strike a firm final blow to the chisel to split the brick. Properly scored bricks split cleanly with one firm blow.

OPTION: When you need to split a lot of bricks uniformly and quickly, use a circular saw fitted with a masonry blade to score the bricks, then split them individually with a chisel. For quick scoring, clamp them securely at each end with a pipe or bar clamp, making sure the ends are aligned. Remember: Wear eye protection when using striking or cutting tools.

How to Angle-cut Brick

1 Mark the final cutting line on the brick. To avoid ruining the brick, you will need to make gradual cuts until you reach this line. Score a straight line for the first cut in the waste area of the brick about ⅛" from the starting point of the final cutting line, perpendicular to the edge of the brick. Make the first cut.

2 Keep the chisel stationary at the point of the first cut, pivot it slightly, then score and cut again. It is important to keep the pivot point of the chisel at the edge of the brick. Repeat until all of the waste area is removed.

How to Cut Brick with a Brick Splitter

1 A brick splitter makes accurate, consistent cuts in bricks and pavers with no scoring required. It is a good idea to rent one if your project requires many cuts. To use the brick splitter, first mark a cutting line on the brick, then set the brick on the table of the splitter, aligning the cutting line with the cutting blade on the tool.

2 Once the brick is in position on the splitter table, pull down sharply on the handle. The cutting blade on the splitter will cleave the brick along the cutting line. TIP: For efficiency, mark cutting lines on several bricks at the same time (see page 69).

How to Cut Concrete Block

1 Mark cutting lines on both faces of the block, then score ⅛" to ¼"-deep cuts along the lines, using a circular saw equipped with a masonry blade.

2 Use a mason's chisel and maul to split one face of the block along the cutting line. Turn the block over and split the other face.

OPTION: Cut half blocks from combination corner blocks. Corner blocks have preformed cores in the center of the web. Score lightly above the core, then rap with a mason's chisel to break off half blocks.

Laying Brick

Patience, care, and good technique are the key elements to building brick structures that have a professional look. Start with a sturdy, level footing (pages 56 to 59), and don't worry if your initial bricklaying attempts aren't perfect. Survey your work often and stop when you spot a problem. As long as the mortar's still soft, you can remove bricks and try again.

This section features one method of brick wall construction: laying up the ends of the wall first, then filling in the interior bricks. The alternate method, laying one course at a time, is shown with concrete block (pages 76 to 79).

Everything You Need:

Tools: Gloves, trowel, chalk line, level, line blocks, mason's string, jointing tool.

Materials: Mortar, brick, wall ties, rebar (optional).

Buttering is a term used to describe the process of applying mortar to the end of a brick or block before adding it to the structure being built. Apply a heavy layer of mortar to one end of a brick, then cut off the excess with a trowel.

How to Build a Double-wythe Brick Wall

1 Dry-lay the first course by setting down two parallel rows of brick, spaced ¾" to 1" apart. Use a chalk line to outline the location of the wall on the slab. Draw pencil lines on the slab to mark the ends of the bricks. Test-fit the spacing with a ⅜"-diameter dowel, then mark the locations of the joint gaps to use as a reference after the spacers are removed.

2 Dampen the concrete slab or footing with water, and dampen the bricks or blocks if necessary (page 69). Mix mortar and throw a layer of mortar on the footing for the first two bricks of one wythe at one end of the layout. Butter the inside end of the first brick, then press the brick into the mortar, creating a ⅜" mortar bed (step 2, page 76). Cut away excess mortar.

3 Plumb the face of the end brick, using a level. Tap lightly with the handle of the trowel to correct the brick if it is not plumb. Level the brick end to end. Butter the end of a second brick (page 72), then set it into the mortar bed, pushing the dry end toward the first brick to create a joint of ⅜".

4 Butter and place a third brick, using the chalk lines as a general reference, then using a level to check for level and plumb. Adjust any bricks that are not aligned by tapping lightly with the trowel handle.

5 Lay the first three bricks for the other wythe, parallel to the first wythe. Level the wythes, and make sure the end bricks and mortar joints align. Fill the gaps between the wythes at each end with mortar.

Header bricks

6 Cut a half brick (page 70 to 71), then throw and furrow a mortar bed for a half brick on top of the first course. Butter the end of the half brick, then set the half brick in the mortar bed, creating a ⅜" joint. Cut away excess mortar. Make sure bricks are plumb and level.

7 Add more bricks and half bricks to both wythes at the end until you lay the first bricks in the fourth course. Align bricks with the reference lines. NOTE: To build corners, lay a header brick at the end of two parallel wythes. Position the header brick in each subsequent course perpendicular to the header brick in the previous course (inset).

(continued next page)

8 Check the spacing of the end bricks with a straight-edge. Properly spaced bricks will form a straight line when you place the straightedge over the stepped end bricks. If bricks are not in alignment, do not move those bricks already set. Try to compensate for the problem gradually as you fill in the middle (field) bricks (Step 9) by slightly reducing or increasing the spacing between the joints.

9 Every 30 minutes, stop laying bricks and smooth out all the untooled mortar joints with a jointing tool. Do the horizontal joints first, then the vertical joints. Cut away any excess mortar pressed from the joints, using a trowel. When the mortar has set, but is not too hard, brush any excess mortar from the brick faces.

Line block

10 Build the opposite end of the wall with the same methods as the first, using the chalk lines as a reference. Stretch a mason's string between the two ends to establish a flush, level line between ends—use line blocks to secure the string. Tighten the string until it is taut. Begin to fill in the field bricks (the bricks between ends) on the first course, using the mason's string as a guide.

11 Lay the remaining field bricks. The last brick, called the closure brick, should be buttered at both ends. Center the closure brick between the two adjoining bricks, then set in place with the trowel handle. Fill in the first three courses of each wythe, moving the mason's string up one course after completing each course.

Metal wall tie

12 In the fourth course, set metal wall ties into the mortar bed of one wythe and on top of the brick adjacent to it. Space the ties 2 to 3 ft. apart, every three courses. For added strength, set metal rebar into the cavities between the wythes and fill with thin mortar (page 68).

13 Lay the remaining courses, installing metal ties every third course. Check with mason's string frequently for alignment, and use a level to make sure the wall is plumb and level.

14 Lay a furrowed mortar bed on the top course, and place a wall cap on top of the wall to cover empty spaces and provide a finished appearance. Remove any excess mortar. Make sure the cap blocks are aligned and level. Fill the joints between cap blocks with mortar.

Laying Block

Block walls can be built fairly quickly because of the size of the individual blocks. Still, the same patience and attention to detail involved in laying bricks are required. Check your work often, and don't be afraid to back up a step or two to correct your mistakes.

This section features a concrete block wall laid up one course at a time. Make sure you have a sturdy, level footing (page 56 to 59) before you start.

Everything You Need:

Tools: Trowel, chalk line, level, mason's string, line blocks, jointing tool.

Materials: Mortar mix, 8 × 8" concrete blocks, stakes, cap blocks, rebar, wire reinforcing strips.

Buttering a concrete block involves laying narrow slices of mortar on the two flanges at the end of the block. It is not necessary to butter the valley between the flanges unless the project calls for it.

How to Lay Concrete Block

1 Dry-lay the first course, leaving a ⅜" gap between blocks (page 66). Draw reference lines on the concrete base to mark the ends of the row, extending the lines well past the edges of the block. Use a chalk line to snap reference lines on each side of the base, 3" from the blocks. These reference lines will serve as a guide when setting the blocks into mortar.

2 Dampen the base slightly, then mix mortar and throw and furrow two mortar lines (pages 28 to 30) at one end to create a mortar bed for the combination corner block. Dampen porous blocks before setting them into the mortar beds (page 69).

3 Set a combination corner block (page 64) into the mortar bed. Press it into the mortar to create a ⅜"-thick bed joint. Hold the block in place and cut away the excess mortar (save excess mortar for the next section of the mortar bed). Check the block with a level to make sure it is level and plumb. Make any necessary adjustments by rapping on the high side with the handle of a trowel. Be careful not to displace too much mortar.

4 Drive a stake at each end of the project and attach one end of a mason's string to each stake. Thread a line level onto the string and adjust the string until it is level and flush with the top of the corner block. Throw a mortar bed and set a corner block at the other end. Adjust the block so it is plumb and level, making sure it is aligned with the mason's string.

5 Throw a mortar bed for the second block at one end of the project: butter one end of a standard block and set it next to the corner block, pressing the two blocks together so the joint between them is ⅜" thick. Tap the block with the handle of a trowel to set it, and adjust the block until it is even with the mason's string. Be careful to maintain the ⅜" joint.

6 Install all but the last block in the first course, working from the ends toward the middle. Align the blocks with the mason's string. Clean excess mortar from the base before it hardens.

(continued next page)

7 Butter the flanges on both ends of a standard block for use as the "closure block" in the course. Slide the closure block into the gap between blocks, keeping the mortar joints an even thickness on each side. Align the block with the mason's string.

8 Apply a 1"-thick mortar bed for the half block at one end of the wall, then begin the second course with a half block.

9 Set the half block into the mortar bed with the smooth surfaces facing out. Use the level to make sure the half block is plumb with the first corner block, then check to make sure it is level. Adjust as needed. Install a half block at the other end.

Vertical joints

VARIATION: If your wall has a corner, begin the second course with a full-sized end block that spans the vertical joint formed where the two walls meet. This layout creates and maintains a running bond for the wall (page 65).

10 Attach a mason's string for reference, securing it either with line blocks (page 74) or a nail. If you do not have line blocks, insert a nail into the wet mortar at each end of the wall, then wind the mason's string around and up to the top corner of the second course, as shown above. Connect both ends and draw the mason's string taut. Throw a mortar bed for the next block, then fill out the second course, using the mason's string as a reference line.

11 Every half-hour, tool the fresh mortar joints with a jointing tool and remove any excess mortar. Tool the horizontal joints first, then the vertical joints. Cut off excess mortar, using a trowel blade. When the mortar has set, but is not too hard, brush any excess mortar from the block faces. Continue building the wall until it is complete.

OPTION: When building stack bond walls with vertical joints that are in alignment, use wire reinforcing strips in the mortar beds every third course (or as required by local codes) to increase the strength of the wall. The wire should be completely embedded in the mortar. See page 68 for other block wall reinforcing options.

12 Install a wall cap (page 64) on top of the wall to cover the empty spaces and create a finished appearance. Set the cap pieces into mortar beds, then butter an end with mortar. Level the cap, then tool to match the joints in the rest of the wall.

Working with stone demands patience and exacting attention to detail. But the rewards are many. Few masonry materials rival stone for spectacular beauty or durability. Consult the section on footings (56 to 59) for general guidance on pouring a footing suitable for your project.

Working with Stone

Building with stone is an enormously satisfying activity for anyone who enjoys developing a craft and doesn't mind hard work. Many issues affecting the ultimate look of your wall, pillar, arch, walk, or other stone project are entirely up to you to decide: Stone masons often prefer to recess the mortar in the joints so the stones—not the mortar—are emphasized. However, you may want to emphasize an attractively tinted mortar by adding extra mortar to the joints. Learn how to use mortar (pages 28 to 31) to create the effect you desire. You can also be creative in the way you "dress" stones for your project, chiseling the faces smooth, or letting them retain their natural look (pages 84 to 87). The following pages show you how to combine age-old techniques with state-of-the-art tools and materials to get the most satisfying results out of your stone work.

Wear a lifting belt to support your back and stomach muscles, and always bend at the knees as you lift stone. If you can't, the stone is too heavy to lift alone. Find a helper, and consider using an alternative technique for moving the stone into position (pages 81 and 88 to 89).

Tips for Working with Stone

Stone work is a labor-intensive craft. Completing a big stone project on your own can take many days. Assemble a team for your project, rotating the responsibilities to keep everyone involved. With five or more working, you can complete many stone projects in a weekend.

Stone weighs 165 lb./cu. ft., on average. This can make it difficult to place stones precisely. There are many good techniques for moving stone safely and effectively (pages 88 to 89). Use ramps and simple lifting or towing devices, such as chains, to simplify the task any time a stone is too heavy to lift comfortably.

Cutting stones to fit is an important part of working with stone (pages 84 to 87). Keep a circular saw equipped with a silicon-carbide masonry blade on hand, along with a maul and chisel. Some stone masons prefer to do all their cutting with a maul and chisel to avoid unnaturally straight lines, but if there's a lot of splitting to do, you may want one person to take the first pass with a saw (called scoring) while another does the final splitting with a maul and chisel.

Organize stones by size and shape before starting your project. Taking the extra time required at the start of a project will save a lot of effort in the long run. If you're building a wall, stack long stones that will serve as tie stones (pages 88 to 89) in one area; filler, or wedge, stones in another area; and the remaining stones in a third.

When choosing stone, you'll need to decide what type and what form to use. If you're shopping at a stone supply yard, you'll also find a wide range of shades and textures.

The most common types of stone for outdoor construction are shown at left. In addition to a distinctive look, each type has a specific durability and workability to consider. If you expect to do a lot of splitting, ask your local stone supplier to help you select stone that splits easily. If you're laying a walk, select stone that holds up well under foot traffic. Cost, of course, is also a factor. Other things being equal, you will find that stone native to your area is the most affordable.

A stone's form can be thought of as its shape or cut. Common forms (right) include ashlar, cobblestone, rubble, fieldstone, flagstone, and veneer stone. Some stone is uncut because its natural shape lends itself to certain types of construction. Stone is cut thin for use as facing stone (veneer) and wall caps (capstone). Often, the project dictates the form of stone to use. For example, most arches require stone with smooth, roughly square sides, such as ashlar, that can be laid up with very thin mortar joints.

Once you've determined the type and form of stone for your project, you can browse the wide range of shades and textures available and decide what best complements the look and feel of your yard.

NOTE: You may find that in your area different terms are used for various types of stone. Ask your supply yard staff to help you.

Limestone – heavy stone, moderately easy to cut, medium to high strength, used in garden walls, rock gardens, walks, steps, and patios. Major U.S. sources: Indiana, Wisconsin, Kansas, and Texas.

Granite – dense, heavy stone, difficult to cut, used for paving walks and building steps and walls; the most widely used building stone. Major U.S. sources: Massachusetts, Georgia, Minnesota, North Carolina, South Dakota, and Vermont.

Sandstone – relatively lightweight stone available in "soft" and "dense" varieties and a wide range of colors. Soft sandstone is easier to cut, but also lower in strength; used in garden walls, especially in frost-free climates. Major U.S. sources: New York, Arizona, Ohio, and Pennsylvania.

Slate – fine, medium-weight stone that is soft and easy to cut, but low in strength; too brittle for wall construction, but a popular choice for walks, steps and patios; colors vary widely from region to region. Major U.S. sources: Pennsylvania, Virginia, Vermont, Maine, New York, and Georgia,

Flagstone – large slabs of quarried stone cut into pieces up to 3" thick; used in walks, steps, and patios. Pieces smaller than 16" sq. are often called *steppers.*

Split fieldstone

Fieldstone – stone gathered from fields, dry river beds, and hillsides; used in wall construction. When split into smaller, more manageable shapes, fieldstone is often used in mortared construction. Called *river rock* by some quarries because of the river-bed origin of some fieldstone.

Rubble – irregular pieces of quarried stone, usually with one split or finished face; widely used in wall construction.

Ashlar – quarried stone smooth-cut into large blocks ideal for creating clean lines with thin mortar joints.

Veneer stone – pieces of natural or manufactured stone, cut or molded for use in non-load-bearing, cosmetic applications, such as facing exterior walls or freestanding concrete block walls.

Cobblestone – small cuts of quarried stone or fieldstone; used in walks and paths.

Cutting & Shaping Stone

You can cut most stone by placing it directly on a bed of flat, soft ground, such as grass or sand, that will absorb some of the shock when the maul strikes the chisel. Use a sandbag for additional support. You can also build a simple cutting platform, called a *banker* (page 85), to support stones in a bed of sand. Protect yourself by wearing safety glasses and heavy gloves and using the proper tools for the job. A standard brickset chisel and hammer are too light, and a carpenter's framing hammer is too light and is made of brittle material that may chip when striking a chisel. The best tools are a pitching chisel (page 85) for long, clean cuts, a pointing chisel (page 85) for removing small bumps, a basic stone chisel (page 85), and a maul for tapping the chisels. A mason's hammer—with its pick at one end—is also useful for breaking off small chips.

It is often helpful to mark a stone for cutting while it sits in place on a wall or other structure, but never cut a stone while it is in place, even to remove a small bump. You risk splitting surrounding stones and breaking the mortar bond, if you're using mortar. For splitting, move the stone to soft ground or a banker at the base of the wall.

Everything You Need:

Tools: Maul, stone chisel, pitching chisel, pointing chisel, mason's hammer, circular saw, silicon-carbide masonry blades, GFCI extension cord.

Materials: Stone, sand, 2 × 2s, wallboard.

Tips for Cutting Stone

Laying stones works best when the sides (including the top and bottom) are roughly square. If a side is sharply skewed, score and split it with a pitching chisel, and chip off smaller peaks with a pointing chisel or mason's hammer. REMEMBER: a stone should sit flat on its bottom or top side without much rocking.

"Dress" a stone, using a pointing chisel and maul, to remove jagged edges or undesirable bumps. Position the chisel at a 30 to 45° angle at the base of the piece to be removed. Tap lightly all around the break line, then more forcefully, to chip off the piece. Position the chisel carefully before each blow with the maul.

Build a banker if you plan on a lot of splitting. This simple sand-bed table provides a sturdy, but shock-absorbent work surface. Place it atop two columns of concrete block if you prefer to stand while splitting. Construct frames out of 2 x 2s, and sandwich a piece of ¾" plywood between the frames. Attach pieces by driving 3½" coarse-threaded wallboard screws through from both sides, and fill it with sand.

Grind the head of a chisel smooth on a grindstone any time the head begins to *mushroom* (curled edges appear). The curling results from repeated blows to the chisel with a maul. Small shards of metal can break free, becoming dangerous projectiles. REMEMBER: Always wear safety goggles when handling cutting tools.

Tips for Cutting Stone with a Circular Saw

A circular saw lets you precut stones with broad surfaces with greater control and accuracy than most people can achieve with a chisel. It's a noisy tool, so wear ear plugs, along with a dust mask and safety goggles. Install a toothless masonry blade on your saw and start out with the blade set to cut ⅛" deep. (Make sure the blade is designed for the material you're cutting. Some masonry blades are designed for hard materials like concrete, marble, and granite. Others are for soft materials, like concrete block, brick, flagstone, and limestone.) Wet the stone before cutting to help control dust, then make three passes, setting the blade ⅛" deeper with each pass. Repeat the process on the other side. A thin piece of wood under the saw protects the saw foot from rough masonry surfaces. REMEMBER: Always use a GFCI outlet or extension cord when using power tools outdoors.

How to Cut Fieldstone

1 Place the stone on a banker, or prop it with sandbags, and mark with chalk or a crayon all the way around the stone, indicating where you want it to split. If possible, use the natural fissures in the stone as cutting lines.

2 Score along the line using moderate blows with a chisel and maul, then strike solidly along the score line with a pitching chisel to split the stone. Dress the stone with a pointing chisel (page 85).

How to Cut Flagstone

1 Trying to split a large flagstone in half can lead to many unpredicted breaks. For best results, chip off small sections at a time. Mark the stone on both sides with chalk or a crayon, indicating where you want it to split. If there is a fissure nearby, mark your line there since that is probably where the stone will break naturally.

2 Score along the line on the back side of the stone (the side that won't be exposed) by moving a chisel along the line and striking it with moderate blows with a maul. OPTION: If you have a lot of cutting to do, reduce hammering fatigue by using a circular saw to score the stones, and a maul and chisel to split them. Keep the stone wet during cutting with a circular saw to reduce dust.

3 Turn the stone over, place a pipe or 2 × 4 directly under the chalk line, then strike forcefully with the maul on the end of the portion to be removed.

OPTION: If a paving stone looks too big compared to other stones in your path, simply set the stone in place and strike a heavy blow to the center with a sledge hammer. It should break into several usable pieces.

Laying Stone

Natural stone is heavy material—about 165 lb./cubic foot on average. So, the first thing to remember when laying stone is to handle it with care so you avoid injury to yourself and others. The methods of laying stone are as varied as the stone masons who practice the craft. But all of them would agree on a few general principles:

- Thinner joints are stronger joints. Whether you are using mortar or dry-laying stone, the more contact between stones, the more resistance to any one stone dislodging.

- *Tie stones* are essential in vertical structures, such as walls or pillars. These long stones span at least two-thirds the width of the structure, tying together the shorter stones around them.

- When working with mortar, most stone masons point their joints deep for aesthetic reasons. The less mortar is visible, the more the stone itself is emphasized.

- Long vertical joints, or *head* joints, are weak spots in a wall. Close the vertical joints by overlapping them with stones in the next course, similar to a running bond pattern in a brick or block wall (page 65).

- The sides of a stone wall should have an inward slope (called *batter*) for maximum strength. This is especially important with dry-laid stone (page 89). Mortared walls need less batter.

Thin joints are the strongest. When working with mortar, joints should be ½-1" thick. Mortar is not intended to create gaps between stones, but to fill the inevitable gaps and strengthen the bonds between stones. Wiggle a stone once it is in place to get it as close as possible to adjoining stones.

Blend large and small stones in walks or in vertical structures to achieve the most natural appearance. In addition to enhancing visual appeal, long stones in a walk act like the tie stones in a wall, adding strength by bonding with other stones.

Place uneven stone surfaces down and dig out the soil underneath until the stone lies flat. Use the same approach in the bottom course of a dry-laid wall, only make sure stones at the base of a wall slope toward the center of the trench (pages 188 to 189).

Tips for Laying Stone in Walls & Other Structures

Tie stones are long stones that span most of the width of a wall (pages 188 to 189), tying together the shorter stones, and increasing the wall's strength. As a guide, figure that 20 percent of the stones in a structure should be tie stones.

A **shiner** is the opposite of a tie stone—a flat stone on the side of a wall that contributes little in terms of strength. A shiner may be necessary when no other stone will fit in a space. Use shiners as seldom as possible, and use tie stones nearby to compensate.

Lay stones in horizontal courses, where possible, a technique called *ashlar* construction. If necessary, stack two to three thin stones to match the thickness of adjoining stones.

With irregular stone, such as untrimmed rubble or field stone, building course by course is difficult. Instead, place stones as needed to fill gaps and to overlap the vertical joints.

Use a batter gauge and level to lay up dry stone structures so the sides slope inward. Slope the sides of a wall 1" for every 2 ft. of height—less for ashlar and free-standing walls, twice as much for round stone and retaining walls.

Working with Tile

With its exceptional durability, outdoor-rated tile is a great decorating material. You can dress up a stoop, resurface a patio, or add color to a concrete walkway, using tile designed for outdoor installation.

There are three important rules to follow for outdoor tile: Use only tile rated for exterior application—one with a surface that won't become slippery when wet—lay the tile over a flat, solid foundation, and seal the grout and the tile (if recommended by the manufacturer), to protect against damage.

The tiling project on pages 158 to 171 shows you how to pour a new concrete slab over an old patio to create a smooth subbase for new tile. You'll also find tips for tiling directly over your patio.

A natural terra-cotta finish and sturdy construction make quarry tile a popular choice for outdoor floors. Whatever floor tile you choose for outdoors, be sure it is designed to withstand annual freeze-thaw cycles.

Tips for Working with Tile

Select tiles for their size, shape, color, and style. Light-colored tiles brighten a surface and can make it appear larger, but they also show dirt more than do dark tiles. Large floor tiles are easier to lay than smaller ones and generally require less maintenance.

Plan your layout carefully. Arrange full tiles in the most visible areas, saving cut tiles for less conspicuous spaces. Adjust the layout so cut tiles are no less than half their original size. Create reference lines to guide your tile installation (step 3, page 165).

Working with Mixed Media

Using information and techniques found in this book, you can combine masonry materials and other elements to create custom accents for your home and garden.

Landscape design offers the greatest opportunity for combining materials in custom designs. By combining manufactured and natural materials, you can bring out the distinctive qualities of each while adding interest to the whole.

Because it can be formed into almost any shape, concrete is useful for mixed media projects. You can embed objects in a concrete surface (pages 118 to 119), imprint the concrete, or use finishing techniques (pages 52 to 53) to achieve a custom texture. Wet stucco and mortar provide similar opportunities for creativity.

Use the ideas here to start thinking about mixed media projects, then look through the book to find projects and techniques that involve specific materials. This can help you determine the compatibility of your selected media and will guide your planning and installation.

Combine materials in visually appealing patterns, as was done in this walkway made from natural stones, brick pavers, and ceramic tiles. When selecting media for outdoor projects, consider how the materials will stand up to weather, outdoor furniture, and heavy foot traffic.

Tips for Working with Mixed Media

Decorate concrete by imprinting the surface with leaves or twigs, or by embedding small objects after screeding the concrete (pages 118 to 119). Trowel powdered pigments and dry cement into the wet concrete surface to give it a distinctive color.

Use natural materials to lend a rustic feel to a concrete walk. This walk mixes smooth and exposed-aggregate concrete (pages 52 to 53). Ashlar stone retaining walls make an effective transition between concrete and plants, shrubs, and soil.

Ingredients of scratch (base) coat, and brown coat stucco

3 parts sand
2 parts portland cement
1 part masonry cement
Water

Ingredients of finish coat stucco

1 part lime
3 parts sand
6 parts white cement
Tint (as desired)
Water

Water

Sand

Portland cement

Lime

Preformulated stucco mix

Combine dry stucco mix with water, following the manufacturer's directions for each coat. For the finish coat, mix a test batch first. Add measured amounts of stucco and tint until you find the proper combination. Record the recipe, so you can replicate it for subsequent batches. A finish coat requires slightly more water than other coats (page 95).

Working with Stucco

Working with stucco is a craft that's been practiced for hundreds of years. Today's stucco is a combination of portland cement, masonry cement, sand, and (in the finish coat) lime, all mixed with water. The dry ingredients are widely available in premixed bags. The mixture is applied to walls and worked with either a trowel or a brush to achieve the desired effect.

Stuccoing an entire house from scratch is a demanding proposition. But repairing or remodeling small sections (pages 278 to 279) is not difficult. Walls that are kept in good condition and "redashed" occasionally with a restorative coat can last for decades.

Stucco can be applied to masonry surfaces, such as concrete block, or over wood or other materials that have been covered with building paper and metal lath. When applying stucco over

brick or block, two coats—a ⅜"-thick base coat and a ¼"-thick finish coat—are applied. Over building paper and metal lath, three coats are applied—a scratch coat (⅜"-½" thick), a brown coat (⅜" thick), and a finish coat (⅛" thick).

Follow manufacturer's instructions regarding drying times between coats.

Everything You Need:

Tools: Cement mixer, mortar hawk, square-end trowel, hammer, stapler, utility knife, aviation snips, shovel, bucket, whisk broom, metal rake.

Materials: 15-lb. weather-resistant building paper, self-furring expanded metal lath, edging, drip screed, 1½" galvanized roofing nails or heavy-duty staples, stucco mix.

Tips for Preparing Surfaces for Stucco

Attach building paper to wood frame construction, using heavy-duty staples or roofing nails. Overlap sheets 4". In some regions, more than one layer of building paper may be required. Ask your local building inspector about code specifications.

Install self-furring expanded metal lath over the paper with 1½" roofing nails, driven into studs every 6". Sheets of lath should overlap 1" horizontally and 2" vertically. Make sure the lath is installed with the rougher side facing out.

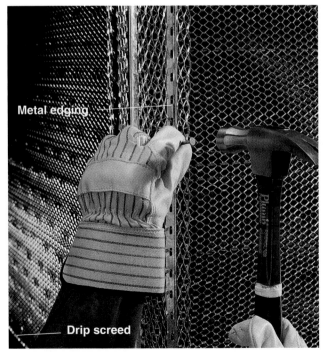

Install metal edging along edges of walls, and drip, or *weep*, screed at the base to achieve clean corners and edges when you apply stucco. Make sure edging is level and plumb, then attach it with roofing nails.

Use aviation snips to trim the excess lath, edging, and drip screed. Wear safety goggles and heavy gloves as protection from sharp edges.

Tips for Preparing Surfaces for Stucco

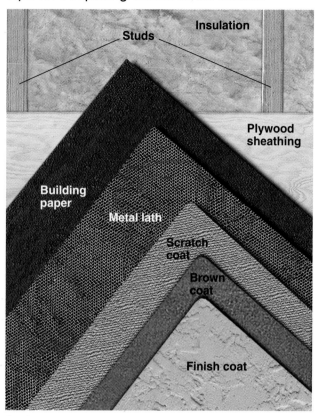

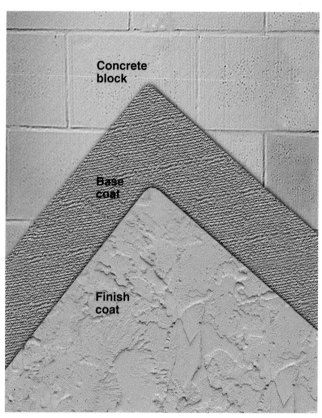

Surface preparation and the number of coats of stucco vary, depending on wall construction. A wood frame construction or insulation board surface must be covered with building paper and lath, then plastered with three coats of stucco. Stucco can be plastered directly onto concrete block, using two coats.

Tips for Applying Stucco

Use a power cement mixer for large projects. Add water to the mix until it forms a workable paste, following manufacturer's instructions.

Begin at the top or the bottom of the wall. Hold a mortar hawk close to the wall, and press stucco into the lath with a square-end trowel. Press firmly to fill voids, and cover the mesh as smoothly as possible.

Tips for Finishing Stucco

Develop a formula that yields a consistent color and texture. Test finish batches first by applying them to a scrap of wood. Let the samples dry for at least an hour, for an indication of their color after the stucco has cured. Record the proper proportions.

Mix the finish batch, so it contains slightly more water than the scratch and brown coats. The mix should still stay on the mortar hawk without running.

Cover a float with carpet to make an ideal tool for achieving a float-finish texture. Experiment on a small area.

Achieve a wet-dash finish by flinging, or *dashing,* stucco onto the surface. Let the stucco cure undisturbed.

For a dash-trowel texture, dash the surface with stucco, using a whisk broom (left), then flatten the stucco by troweling over it.

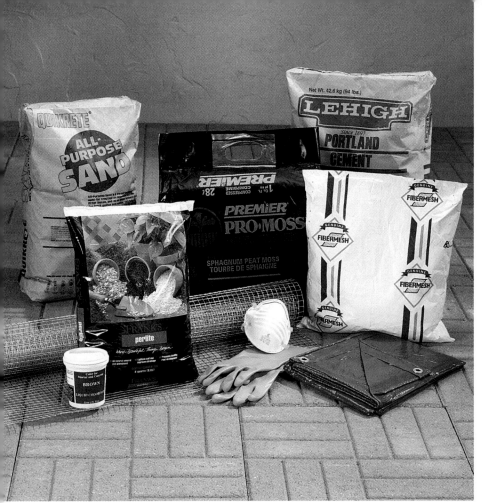

The materials for making hypertufa are inexpensive and widely available. They include portland cement, perlite, peat moss, fiberglass fibers, mason's sand, concrete tint, hardware cloth, a plastic tarp, a dust mask, and rubber gloves.

Recipe #1

2 buckets portland cement
3 buckets sifted peat moss
3 buckets perlite
1 handful of fiberglass fibers
Powdered concrete tint (optional)

Mix cement, peat moss, and perlite in wheelbarrow or mixing trough. Add fiberglass fibers and tint (as required). Mix until the fibers are evenly distributed through the mixture.

Add water, a little at a time, and mix it in thoroughly. When you can pick up a handful of the mix and squeeze out a few drops of water, it's ready to be formed.

Recipe #2

3 buckets portland cement
3 buckets mason's sand
3 buckets sifted peat moss
Powdered concrete tint (optional)

Mix dry directions thoroughly, as above. Add small amounts water until the mix has the consistency of cottage cheese.

Working with Hypertufa

Hypertufa is a masonry material that contains peat moss, and is well suited to building planters, pedestals, and birdbaths that have a rustic appeal. Wet hypertufa is packed into forms, and then cured.

Two recipes for hypertufa are included above, one containing fiberglass fibers, for a lightweight, durable mixture—ideal for medium-to-large planting containers; the other containing sand, for smaller items and those that must hold water. All of the ingredients are available at home and garden centers.

Use pure portland cement, rather than prepared concrete mix, which adds unnecessary weight and gives the finished container a coarse texture. In Recipe #1, perlite, a soil lightener, takes the place of conventional aggregate. For Recipe #2, use fine-textured mason's sand—it produces a stronger container than coarser grades.

Peat moss naturally includes a range of textures, some of which are too coarse for hypertufa. Sifting the peat moss through hardware cloth takes care of that problem. If you plan to make several hypertufa pieces, buy a large bale of peat moss, sift the entire bale, then store the sifted material for use over time.

Recipe #1 calls for loose fiberglass fibers that contribute strength to the mixture. This product is available at most home centers, but if you have trouble locating it, try a masonry supply center.

Hypertufa naturally dries to the color of concrete. If you prefer another color, add a powdered concrete tint during the mixing process. Tinting products are highly concentrated, so start with a small amount and add more if necessary.

How to Prepare & Pour Hypertufa

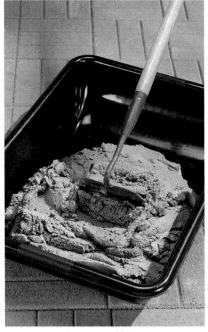

1 Place hardware cloth across the top of a large bucket or wheelbarrow. Rub the peat moss across the hardware cloth, sifting it through the mesh of the cloth. Discard any remaining particles.

2 Combine measured amounts of the required ingredients for your recipe (page 96). Mix with water until the material reaches the required consistency.

3 Pack hypertufa into forms made of polystyrene insulation held together with gaffer's tape and deck screws (pages 225 and 228). Tamp the material and add more alternately until the material reaches the required depth (pages 224 to 227). Cover with plastic for 48 hours.

4 Disassemble the forms and remove the piece to cure. If the hypertufa includes fiberglass, let it cure, then burn off the exposed fibers, using a light sweeping motion with a propane torch. Apply masonry sealer to basins or other pieces that will hold water.

Tips for Curing Hypertufa

Curing hypertufa properly takes time. Wrap the piece in plastic and put it in a cool place for about a month. Next, unwrap the piece and let it cure outside, uncovered, for several weeks. If you're building a planter, periodically rinse it with water mixed with vinegar to reduce the hypertufa's alkalinity and protect plants. Once the piece has cured outside for several weeks, move it to a dry spot inside, to cure for several more weeks.

Masonry Projects

Masonry Projects

Here are some examples of the spectacular step-by-step projects contained in the pages that follow. Each group of projects in this section of the book is introduced with information about landscaping and specialty tools and techniques. For additional information on working with masonry materials, turn to Basic Techniques, beginning on page 24.

Walks & Paths & Steps (pages 102 to 139)

You can build walks, paths, and steps with a wide variety of materials, from natural flagstone to brick pavers and precast concrete forms. For a path that is simple to build and has a rustic appeal, you can set flagstones or pavers directly in the soil over a bed of crushed stone. Stones, pavers, and other masonry materials that have been set in mortar offer a more formal look. You'll need additional tools and materials and at least a full day to build mortar-set or poured concrete walks, paths, or steps, but the results will be impressive and can last for many years.

Landings, Patios & Driveways (pages 140 to 175)

Patios are among the most popular masonry projects. Once you've built a patio, building a driveway or any other slab will be easier because the projects require many of the same techniques. Several projects in this section show you how to create a new landing, walkway, or patio by building over an existing concrete slab. As long as the original concrete is structurally sound, you can pour fresh concrete or lay pavers or tiles over the original surface.

Walls, Pillars & Arches (pages 176 to 207)

Whether you plan to build a simple wall or something more ambitious, the basic techniques are the same. Arch projects require patience, and a few additional techniques. You'll also need to build a simple wood form to support the structure until it cures.

Finishing House & Garden Walls (pages 208 to 221)

Masonry offers many attractive ways to finish the exterior walls of a house, garage or shed, or to give garden walls a fresh look. Brick, stone, stucco, and surface bonding cement are ideal veneer materials because they offer excellent protection from weather, and require very little maintenance.

Outdoor Accents (pages 222 to 239)

This section mixes some age-old materials, such as the limestone used in this driveway marker (right), with newer materials, such as hypertufa, used in birdbaths, planters, and other attractive garden accessories (below). These projects will add visual interest to the landscape around your home.

Flagstone walkways combine charm with durability and work well in casual or formal settings. Flagstone is also a popular material for patios, and can be set in sand or mortared in place (pages 120 to 121). TIP: Prevent damage to the edging material by trimming near the walkway with a line-feed trimmer instead of a mower.

Walks, Paths & Steps

Walkways and paths serve as "hallways" between heavily used areas of your yard and entryways to your home. They can be used to direct traffic or to guide you toward a favorite landscape feature, such as a pond or flower bed. They can also create a visual corridor that directs the eye from one area to another.

Curved paths have a softer, more relaxed effect. Straight or angular routes fit well in contemporary landscape designs.

Garden paths often are made from loose materials, such as crushed rock, held in place by edging. Walkways are more durable when made from stone or brick paving materials set in sand

or mortar. Poured concrete sidewalks are practical and extremely durable. Most paving techniques used in patio construction (pages 140 to 171) can be used for walkways as well.

A frost footing is not required under walk, paths, or steps, but you will need to remove sod and excavate the site for most projects. The depth of the excavation varies from project to project and depends on the thickness of the masonry material, plus the thickness of the sand or compactible gravel subbase. The subbase provides a more stable surface than the soil itself and an opportunity for water to run off so it does not pool directly under the masonry.

Tips for Building a Walkway

Use a sod cutter to strip grass from your pathway site. Available at most rental centers, sod cutters excavate to a very even depth. The cut sod can be replanted in other parts of your lawn.

Install stakes and strings when laying out straight walkways, and measure from the strings to ensure straight sides and uniform excavation depth.

Options for Directing Water off Walkways

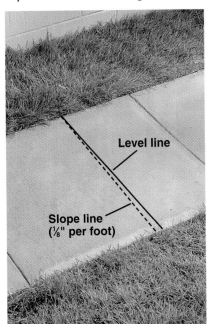

Level line

Slope line (⅛" per foot)

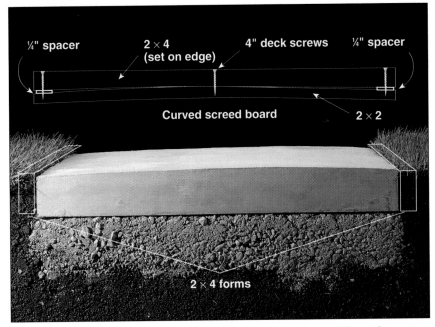

¼" spacer   2 × 4 (set on edge)   4" deck screws   ¼" spacer

Curved screed board   2 × 2

2 × 4 forms

Slope walkways away from the house to prevent water damage to the foundation or basement. Outline the location of the walkway with level mason's strings, then lower the outer string to create a slope of ⅛" per foot (see pages 37 to 39).

Crown the walkway so it is ¼" higher at the center than at the edges. This will prevent water from pooling on the surface. To make the crown, construct a curved screed board by cutting a 2 × 2 and a 2 × 4 long enough to rest on the walkway forms. Butt them together edge to edge and insert a ¼" spacer between them at each end. Attach the parts with 4" deck screws driven at the center and the edges. The 2 × 2 will be drawn up at the center, creating a curved edge. Screed the concrete with the curved edge of the screed board facing down.

Brick edging: Loose material, Landscape fabric, Brick edging

Brick edging makes a good boundary for both straight and curved paths made from loose materials.

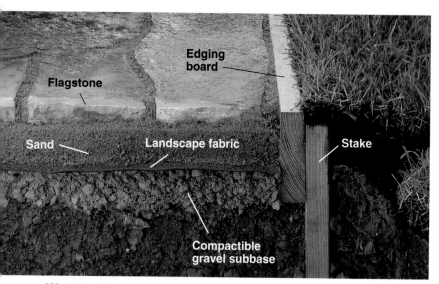

Wood edging: Flagstone, Edging board, Sand, Landscape fabric, Stake, Compactible gravel subbase

Wood edging makes a sturdy border for straight walkways made from flagstone or brick pavers set in sand.

Rigid plastic edging: Brick pavers, Rigid plastic edging, Sand, Landscape fabric, Compactible gravel subbase

Rigid plastic edging installs easily, and works well for both curved and straight walkways made from paving stones or brick pavers set in sand.

Laying a Loose-fill Path

You can use edging to keep walkway materials in place and to add a more finished look. Consider cost, appearance, flexibility, and ease of installation when selecting an edging type.

Brick edging set in soil is good for casual, lightly traveled pathways, but should be used only in soil that is dense and well drained. (In loose or swampy soil bricks will not hold their position.) Bricks can be set vertically, or tilted at an angle to make a saw-tooth pattern. Brick pavers also can be mortared to the sides of an old sidewalk to create a border for a new surface (steps 2 to 4, page 114).

Wood edging made from pressure-treated lumber, redwood or cedar is inexpensive and easy to install. The tops of boards are left exposed to create an attractive border. The wood edging boards are held in place by attaching them to recessed wood stakes spaced every 12" along the outside of the edging.

Rigid plastic edging is inconspicuous, durable, and easy to install. It was developed as an edging for brick pavers set in sand. Rigid plastic edging is held in place by the weight of the soil along with galvanized spikes driven through the back flange. Rolled vinyl edging works as an edging for casual walkways as well as planting areas. It is inexpensive and flexible.

Everything You Need:

Tools: Garden hose or rope, spade, hoe, or rented saw cutter, rake, rubber mallet.

Materials: Landscape fabric, bricks, gravel, crushed rock, bark, or wood chips, 1 × 4 lumber.

How to Build a Path Using Loose Materials & Brick Edging

1 Outline the path, using a garden hose or rope (page 12), then excavate the site to a depth of 2" to 3", using a spade, hoe, or a rented sod cutter (page 103). Rake the site smooth.

2 Dig narrow edging trenches, about 2" deeper than the path site, along both edges of the excavation, using a spade or hoe.

3 Lay landscaping fabric between the edging trenches to prevent weeds. Overlap sheets by at least 6".

4 Set bricks on end into the edging trenches, with the tops slightly above ground level. Pack soil behind and beneath each brick, adjusting the bricks, if necessary, to keep the rows even.

5 Finish the path by spreading loose material (gravel, crushed rock, bark, or wood chips) between the rows of edging bricks. Level the surface with a garden rake. The loose material should be slightly above ground level. Tap each brick lightly on the inside face to help set it into the soil. Inspect and adjust the bricks yearly, adding new loose material as needed.

Pouring a Concrete Walkway

Pouring a concrete walkway is one of the most practical projects you can master as a homeowner. Once you've excavated and poured a walkway, you can confidently take on larger concrete projects, such as patios and driveways.

This project shows you how to lay out the site (including any turns you want to incorporate), excavate and build forms, lay down a gravel subbase, and pour and work the concrete. For more information on these steps, and the most effective techniques, consult the section on concrete in Basic Techniques (pages 34 to 61).

Everything You Need:

Tools: Line level, hammer, shovel, sod cutter, wheelbarrow, tamper, drill, level, screed board, straightedge, mason's string, mason's float, mason's trowel, edger, groover, stiff-bristle broom.

Materials: Garden stakes, rebar, bolsters, 2 × 4 lumber, 2½" and 3" screws, concrete mix, concrete sealer, isolation board, compactible gravel, construction adhesive, nails.

How to Build a Walkway

1 Select a rough layout, including any turns. Stake out the location and connect the stakes with mason's strings. Set the slope, if needed (pages 38 to 39). Remove sod between and 6" beyond the lines, then excavate the site with a spade to a depth 4" greater than the thickness of the concrete walkway, following the slope lines to maintain consistent depth (page 39).

2 Pour a 5" layer of compactible gravel as a subbase for the walkway. Tamp the subbase until it compacts to an even 4" thick layer (page 39).

3 Build and install 2 × 4 forms set on edge (page 40). Miter-cut the ends at angled joints. Position them so the inside edges are lined up with the strings. Attach the forms with 3" deck screws, then drive 2 × 4 stakes next to the forms at 3-ft. intervals. Attach the stakes to the forms with 2½" deck screws. Use a level to make sure forms are level or set to achieve the desired slope. Drive stakes at each side of angled joints.

4 Glue an isolation board (page 37) to the steps, house foundation, or other permanent structures that adjoin the walkway, using construction adhesive.

OPTION: Reinforce the walkway with #3 steel rebar (page 41). For a 3-ft.-wide walkway, lay two sections of rebar spaced evenly inside the project area. Use bolsters to support the rebar (make sure rebar is at least 2" below the tops of the forms). Bend rebar to follow any angles or curves, and overlap pieces at angled joints by 12". Mark locations for control joints (to be cut with a groover later) by tacking nails to the outside faces of the forms, spaced roughly at 3-ft. intervals (step 5, page 40).

(continued next page)

5 Mix, then pour concrete into the project area (pages 42 to 47). Use a masonry hoe to spread it evenly within the forms. After pouring all of the concrete, run a spade along the inside edges of the form, then rap the outside edges of the forms with a hammer to help settle the concrete.

6 Build a curved screed board (page 103) and use it to form a crown when you smooth out the concrete. NOTE: A helper makes this easier.

7 Smooth the surface with a float (page 49). Cut control joints at marked locations (page 48) using a trowel and a straightedge. Let the concrete dry until any bleed water disappears (page 49).

8 Shape the edges of the concrete by running an edger along the forms. Smooth out any marks created by the edger, using a float. Lift the leading edges of the edger and float slightly as you work.

9 Once any bleed water has disappeared, draw a groover along the control joints, using a straight 2 × 4 as a guide. Use a float to smooth out any tool marks.

10 Create a textured, non-skid surface by drawing a clean, stiff-bristled broom across the surface (page 52). If you choose a simulated flagstone or brick paver finish, see pages 110-111. Avoid overlapping broom marks. Cover the walkway with plastic and let the concrete cure for one week (page 52).

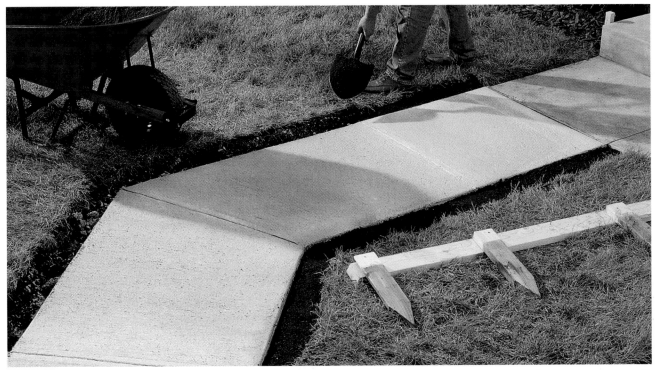

11 Remove the forms, then backfill the space at the sides of the walkway with dirt or sod. Seal the concrete, if desired (pages 54 to 55), according to the manufacturer's directions.

Simulating Flagstones in a Concrete Walkway

Carving joints in a concrete walk is an easy way to simulate the look of natural flagstones and add interest to an otherwise undistinguished path. By tinting the concrete before pouring it and carving the joints, you can create a walk that resembles a tightly laid flagstone path, hence the name *false flagstone* often given to this age-old finishing technique.

Start by studying some flagstone paths in your neighborhood and sketching on paper the look you want to recreate. This way, you can also get an idea of the color to aim for when tinting the concrete mix. Keep in mind the color of your house and landscaping, and experiment with tint until you find a complementary hue. For directions on pouring a concrete walk, turn to the walkway project (pages 106 to 109). For maximum traction, use the brooming technique (page 52).

Give a freshly poured concrete walk the appearance of a natural flagstone path by cutting lines in the surface after floating, then refloating the surface for a durable finish.

Everything You Need:

Tools: Jointing tool or curved ¾" copper pipe, screed board, magnesium float.

Materials: 2 × 4 lumber, concrete mix, tint, concrete sealer.

How to Simulate Flagstones in a Concrete Walkway

1 Pour concrete into forms according to the basic walk-building technique (pages 106 to 109), and smooth the surface with a screed board and magnesium float.

2 Cut shallow lines in the concrete, using a jointing tool or a curved copper pipe. Refloat the surface, and remove the forms once the concrete has cured. Protect the surface with a clear concrete sealer (pages 54 to 55).

Simulating Brick Pavers in a Concrete Walkway

An alternative to the simulated-flagstone technique (page 110) is to pour your walk in sections, using a patterned mold to create either a brick paver or stepping stone effect. You won't need to set up forms for this project—the mold shapes the concrete as you place it. Once you've staked out your site and poured a subbase (pages 106 to 107), you can go right to placing the concrete in the mold. But you will need to take extra care each time you place the mold to make sure the walk follows the path you intended. As with the "false flagstone" project (page 110), you may want to tint the concrete before pouring to recreate the tones of natural stone or pavers. Turn to the related sections for directions on excavating your site (pages 38 to 39), and estimating, mixing and pouring concrete (pages 42 to 47). For maximum traction, use the brooming technique (page 52).

Everything You Need:

Tools: Trowels, concrete mold, shovel.

Materials: Concrete mix, tint, isolation board, compactible gravel, concrete sealer, mason's sand, mortar.

Pour fresh concrete into plastic molds to create slabs with the appearance of neatly arrayed brick pavers. Molds are available for creating "bricks" or "stones" of various shapes and sizes.

How to Use Concrete Paving Molds

1 Place the mold at the start of your excavated site. Fill each mold cavity, and smooth the surface flush with the top of the mold, using a trowel. Let bleed water dry (page 49), then lift the mold and set it aside.

2 Smooth the edges of the concrete with a trowel, adding concrete to fill voids. To pour subsequent sections, place the mold with the same orientation or rotate it ¼ turn. Continue to place and fill the mold until you reach the end of the walk. In the final placement, fill as many cavities as required to reach the walk's edge. Wait a week, then apply clear concrete sealer (pages 54 to 55). Option: Finish the walk by filling the joints with sand or dry mortar (steps 29 to 30, page 153).

Resurfacing a Concrete Walkway

New surface

Old surface

Shown cutaway

Resurface concrete that has surface damage, such as spalling or popouts. Because the new surface will be thin (1" to 2"), use sand-mix concrete. If you are having ready-mix concrete delivered by a concrete contractor, make sure they do not use aggregate larger than ½" in the mixture.

Concrete that has surface damage but is still structurally sound can be preserved by resurfacing—applying a thin layer of new concrete over the old surface. If the old surface has deep cracks or extensive damage, resurfacing will only solve the problem temporarily. Because new concrete will bond better if it is packed down, use a dry, stiff concrete mixture that can be compacted with a shovel.

For a more dramatic change, you can turn an old concrete walkway into a mortared brick path (pages 114 to 115). In this project, mortar applied over the old concrete provides a level foundation for the new brick surface.

How to Resurface Using Fresh Concrete

1 Clean the surface thoroughly. If the surface is flaking or spalled, scrape it with a spade to dislodge as much loose concrete as you can, then sweep the surface clean.

2 Dig a 6"-wide trench around the surface on all sides to create room for 2 × 4 forms.

Everything You Need:

Tools: Shovel, wood float, broom, circular saw, maul, drill, paint brush, paint roller and tray, wheelbarrow, screed board, groover, edger, hose, bricklayer's trowel, jointer, rubber mallet, level, mortar bag.

Materials: Stakes, 2 × 4 lumber, vegetable oil or commerical release agent, 4" wallboard screws, sand-mix concrete, bonding adhesive, plastic sheets, brick pavers, Type N mortar.

3 Stake 2 × 4 forms flush against the sides of the concrete slabs, 1" to 2" above the surface (make sure height is even). Drive stakes every 3 ft. and at every joint in forms. Mark control joint locations onto the outside of the forms directly above existing control joints. Coat the inside edges of the forms with vegetable oil or commercial release agent.

4 Apply a thin layer of bonding adhesive over the entire surface. Follow the directions on the bonding adhesive product carefully. Instructions for similar products may differ slightly.

5 Mix concrete (page 42 to 44), using sand-mix concrete. Make the mixture slightly stiffer (drier) than normal concrete. Spread the concrete, then press down on the concrete with a shovel or 2 × 4 to pack the mixture into the forms. Smooth the surface with a screed board.

6 Float the concrete with a wood float, then tool with an edger, and cut control joints (page 49) in the original locations. Recreate any surface treatment, such as brooming (page 52), used on the original surface. Let the surface cure for one week, covered with plastic. Seal the concrete (page 54).

How to Install Brick Pavers over Concrete

1 Select a paver pattern (pages 64 to 65). Dig a trench around the concrete, slightly wider than the thickness of one paver. Dig the trench so it is about 3½" below the concrete surface. Soak the pavers with water (dry pavers absorb moisture, weakening the mortar strength).

2 Sweep the old concrete, then hose off the surface and sides with water to clear away dirt and debris. Mix a small batch of mortar according to manufacturer's directions. For convenience, place the mortar on a scrap of plywood.

3 Install edging bricks by applying a 1½" layer of mortar to the side of the concrete slab and to one side of each brick. Set bricks into the trench, against the concrete. Brick edging should be 1½" higher than the thickness of the brick pavers.

4 Finish the joints on the edging bricks with a jointer (step 9), then mix and apply a ½"-thick bed of mortar to one end of the sidewalk, using a trowel. Mortar hardens very quickly, so work in sections no larger than 4 sq. ft.

5 Make a "screed" for smoothing mortar by notching the ends of a short 2 × 4 to fit between the edging bricks. Depth of the notches should equal the thickness of the pavers. Drag the screed across the mortar bed until the mortar is smooth.

6 Lay the paving bricks one at a time into the mortar, maintaining a ½" gap between pavers. (A piece of scrap plywood works well as a spacing guide.) Set the pavers by tapping them lightly with a rubber mallet.

7 As each section of pavers is completed, check with a level to make sure the tops of the pavers are even.

8 When all the pavers are installed, use a mortar bag to fill the joints between the pavers with fresh mortar. Work in 4-sq.-ft. sections, and avoid getting mortar on the tops of the pavers.

9 Use a jointer to finish the joints as you complete each 4-sq.-ft. section. For best results, finish the longer joints first, then the shorter joints. Use a trowel to remove excess mortar.

10 Let the mortar dry for a few hours, then remove any residue by scrubbing the pavers with a coarse rag and water. Cover the walkway with plastic and let the mortar cure for at least two days. Remove plastic, but do not walk on pavers for at least one week.

The most basic form of masonry is laying stepping-stones artfully on beds of crushed gravel. As simple as this is, it adds greatly to a landscape's character. A stepping-stone path can be a straight, uniform walkway or a magical, meandering passage, such as this slate path leading into the woods.

Laying a Stepping-stone Path

Whether you are paving a frequently traveled area, or introducing a sense of movement to your landscape, laying a stepping-stone path is an attractive and inexpensive way to add a walkway. Thoughtfully arranged stepping-stones beckon you to walk on them, and, depending on the stones you chose, a stepping-stone path can complement just about any landscape.

When designing your path, keep in mind that paths with gentle curves and balanced placement of large and small stones are often more appealing than straight paths of uniform stones. The distance between stones is also important; set the stones so you can step effortlessly from one to the next.

A variety of path materials are available, from natural stone to prefabricated concrete pavers. Select the material that suits the existing elements in your yard. Stone native to your area is often a good choice (pages 82 to 83). Many stone yards sell 1"- to 2½"-thick rough-cut sedimentary rock "steppers" that are ideal for paths.

For a less rustic look, use square-cut flagstone or pavers.

Even if your path is intended more for decoration than for heavy traffic, keep safety in mind as you design your project. Select stones that are wide enough to stand on comfortably, with surfaces that are flat, even, and lightly textured for traction.

Like other paved surfaces, stepping-stones can be affected by the weather. Without a proper base, they can become unstable or settle unevenly. Prepare the base carefully and check the path each spring, adjusting stones as necessary for safety.

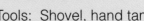

Everything You Need:

Tools: Shovel, hand tamper.

Materials: Sand, stepping-stones.

116

How to Create a Stepping-stone Path

1 Position the stepping-stones on top of the grass and walk along the path to test the layout. Adjust the stones as necessary so you can walk along the path with an effortless stride.

2 Leave the stones in place for three to five days to kill the grass or ground cover underneath. This makes for easier digging and conveniently marks the outline of each stone.

3 Dig up the outlined areas, at least 2" deeper than the thickness of the stones. Spread a 2" layer of sand in each hole. If the stones are of varying thicknesses, adjust with the amount of sand you place in each hole.

4 Reposition the stones, adding or removing sand as necessary until the stones lie flat. Stand on each stone and rock back and forth. Each stone should lie solidly in its bed without rocking.

OPTION: You can give your path a head start on a time-worn look by planting a low-lying spreading ground cover between stones. The ground cover adds contrast and texture and quickly creates the sense of a path that is an integral part of the landscape. Here are a few plants that work well around stepping stones: alyssum, rock cress, thrift, miniature dianthus, candytuft, lobelia, forget-me-not, saxifrage, sedum, thymus, Scotch moss, Irish moss, woolly thyme, and mock strawberry.

A stepping-stone can be as ornate as you want to make it, depending on the materials you use. Homemade stepping-stones can imitate almost any type of stone and can include embedded stones, ceramics, and stamped images that give each stone a unique character.

Making Your Own Stepping-stones

Making stepping-stones from scratch is easy and the materials are readily available. Since you can color the concrete mix with tint available at your local home center, you can make stones of just about any color. All you need is fast-setting concrete mix and some containers you can find in your home. Figure one 40-lb. bag of concrete mix for each 18" × 18" stone. Remember that the mix is caustic: wear a dust mask and rubber gloves when mixing, pouring, and working the material, and wash any residue off your skin with a mild detergent.

Experiment with textures, patterns and shapes. If you don't like a pattern, smooth the surface and start again. However, avoid overworking the surface, which weakens the concrete. And keep in mind that fast-setting concrete sets up in 20 to 40 minutes. To slow the drying process, mist the surface lightly with water after erasing a pattern.

For a more textured look and excellent traction, spread small aggregate over the surface after screeding. Other decorative options include embedding smooth pieces of broken china or pottery.

Depending on the weather in your area, you may want to bring your homemade stones inside during the winter or seal them with concrete sealer (pages 54 to 55).

Everything You Need:

Tools: Bucket, mason's trowel, float, edger, shovel.

Materials: Forms (pie tins, plastic saucers or lids, shallow cardboard or plywood boxes), vegetable oil or commercial release agent, fast-setting concrete mix, stones, pottery shards, or decorative stamps, 1 × 4, sand.

How to Make Your Own Stepping-stones

1 Construct forms or select containers that are 1½" to 2" deep and 12" to 18" square. Coat the forms with vegetable oil, covering the corners and edges. Combine concrete mix, water, and tint (as desired), according to manufacturer's instructions. Adjust the mix so it holds its shape when squeezed. Fill the forms with concrete. Screed the top with a 1 × 4 to fill in gaps and remove excess concrete. Float the surfaces smooth once any bleed water is dry (page 49).

2 Press stones, worn glass or other ornaments into the surface, partially submerging them. Press the ornaments down until you're sure they're firmly set into the stone. Shape the edges, as desired, using a trowel or edger. Let the stepping-stones dry overnight, then remove them from the molds.

3 Dry-lay the stones, then dig beds at least 2" deeper than the thickness of the stones. Spread a 2" layer of sand in each hole. Compensate for differences in stone thickness by adjusting the amount of sand in each hole.

Option: While the surface is still damp, press in ornaments, such as leaves, twigs, shells, or stones, then remove them. Or use decorative rubber stamps to create imprints.

Laying a Flagstone Walkway

With flagstone, sand, and wood edging, you can create a walkway that is durable enough to withstand heavy traffic while maintaining a natural ambience. You can pave a flagstone walkway from start to finish in less than a day. The only maintenance for a sand-set flagstone walkway involves sweeping new sand into the joints every year or two to compensate for erosion and settling.

Everything You Need:

Tools: Garden rake, drill, maul, pitching chisel, circular saw with masonry blade, rubber mallet.

Materials: 2 × 6 lumber (pressure-treated lumber, redwood or cedar), pressure-treated wood stakes, 2½" galvanized screws, compactible gravel, landscape fabric, mason's sand, flagstone.

Test-fit flagstone to find an attractive arrangement that minimizes the amount of splitting required. Leave ⅜" to 2" gaps between stones. Use chalk to mark stones for cutting, then remove the stones and split them, as needed, on a flat surface (pages 84 to 87).

How to Build a Flagstone Walkway

1 Outline the walkway site and excavate to a depth of 6". Allow enough room for the edging and stakes (step 2). For straight walkways, use stakes and strings to maintain a uniform outline. Add a 2" layer of compactible gravel subbase, using a rake to smooth the surface.

2 Install 2 × 6 edging made from pressure-treated lumber around the sides of the site. Drive 12" stakes on the outside of the edging, spaced 12" apart. The tops of the stakes should be below ground level. Attach the edging to the stakes, using galvanized screws.

3 Lay sheets of landscape fabric over the walkway site to prevent weeds and grass from growing up between the stones. (Omit the landscape fabric if you want to plant grass seed or ground cover to fill the cracks). Spread a 2" layer of sand over the landscape fabric to serve as a base for the flagstones.

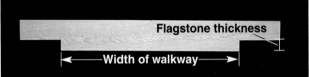

Flagstone thickness

Width of walkway

4 Make a screed board for smoothing the sand by notching the ends of a short 2 × 6 to fit inside the edging (bottom photo). The depth of the notches should equal the thickness of the stones, usually about 2". Screed the base by pulling the 2 × 6 from one end of the walkway to the other. Add more sand as needed until the base is smooth.

5 Beginning at one corner of the walkway, lay the flagstones onto the sand base so the gap between stones is at least ⅜", but no more than 2". If needed, add or remove sand beneath stones to level them. Set the stones by tapping them with a rubber mallet or a length of 2 × 6.

6 Fill the gaps between stones with sand. (Use soil if you are planting grass or ground cover in the cracks.) Pack the sand with your fingers or a piece of scrap wood, then spray the walkway lightly with water to help the sand settle. Add new sand as necessary until gaps are filled.

Simple garden steps can be built by making a series of concrete platforms framed with 5 × 6 timbers. Garden steps have shorter vertical risers and deeper horizontal treads than the outdoor stairs that lead to the threshold of your home. Risers for garden stairs should be no more than 6", and treads should be at least 11" deep.

Building Garden Steps

Garden steps make sloping yards safer and more accessible. They also introduce new combinations of materials into your landscape.

You can build garden steps with a variety of materials, including flagstones, brick, timbers, concrete block, or poured concrete. Whatever materials you use, make sure the steps are level and firmly anchored so they're easy to climb and offer good traction. If you're finishing the steps with concrete, review "Finishing & Curing Concrete" (pages 52 to 53) before you begin pouring.

Everything You Need:

Tools: Maul, chain saw or reciprocating saw with 12" wood-cutting blade, tape measure, level, mason's string, hammer, shovel, drill with 1" spade bit and bit extension, garden rake, mason's trowel, wheelbarrow, mason's hoe, carpenter's square, float, edging tool, stiff-bristle brush.

Materials: 1 × 4 lumber, 1" screws, 5 × 6 landscape timbers, ¾" interior dia. black pipe, 12" galvanized spikes, concrete mix, compactible gravel, seed gravel (½" max. dia.), 2 × 4 board, plastic sheeting, burlap.

Tips for Mixing Concrete

For large amounts (more than ½ cu. yd.), you can mix your own concrete in a wheelbarrow or rented mixer. Use a ratio of 1 part portland cement (A), 2 parts sand (B), and 3 parts gravel (C). See page 43 to estimate the amount of concrete needed.

For small amounts (less than ½ cu. yd.), buy pre-mixed bags of dry concrete (pages 42 to 43). A 60-lb. bag of concrete mix yields about ½ cu. ft. of concrete. A masonry hoe with holes in the blade is useful for mixing concrete (page 18).

Tips for Building Garden Steps

⅛" downward pitch per foot

Build a slight downward pitch into outdoor steps so water will drain off without puddling. Do not exceed a pitch of ⅛" per foot.

Order custom-cut timbers to reduce installation time if the dimensions of each step are identical. Some building supply centers charge a small fee for custom-cutting timbers.

How to Plan Garden Steps

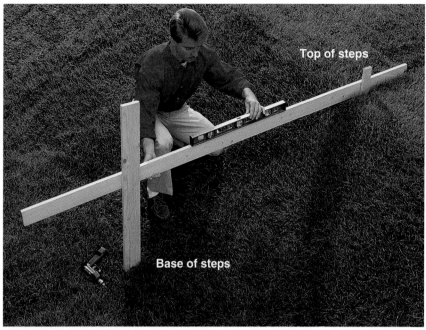

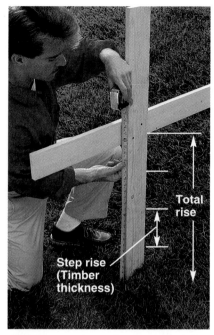

1 Drive a tall stake into the ground at the base of the stairway site. Adjust the stake so it is exactly plumb. Drive a shorter stake at the top of the site. Position a long, straight 1 × 4 against the stakes, with one end touching the ground next to the top stake. Adjust the 1 × 4 so it is level, then attach it to the stakes with screws. (For long spans, use a mason's string instead of a 1 × 4.)

2 Measure from the ground to the bottom of the 1 × 4 to find the total vertical rise of the stairway. Divide the rise by the actual thickness of the timbers (about 6" if using 5 × 6 timbers) to find the number of steps required. Round off any fractions.

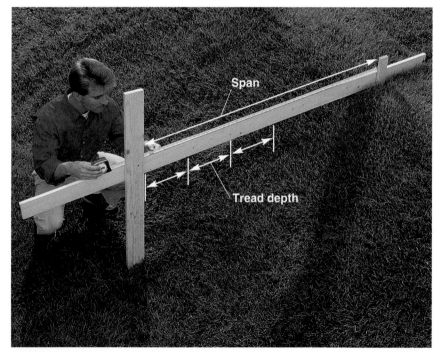

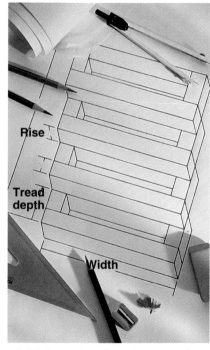

3 Measure along the 1 × 4 between the stakes to find the total horizontal span. Divide the span by the number of steps to find the depth of each step tread. If depth is less than 11", revise the step layout to extend the depth of the step treads.

4 Make a sketch of the step site, showing rise, tread depth, and width of each step. Remember that actual timber dimensions may vary from the nominal measurements.

How to Build Garden Steps Using Timbers & Concrete

1 Mark the sides of the step site with stakes and string. The stakes should be positioned at the front edge of the bottom step and the back edge of the top step.

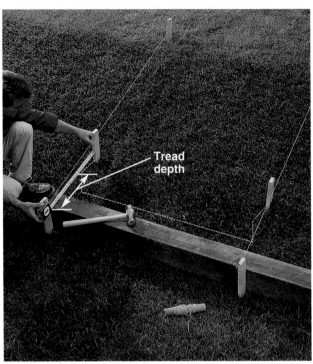

2 Add the width of a timber (about 5") to the tread depth, then measure back this distance from the stakes and drive additional stakes to mark the back edge of the first step. Connect these stakes with string to mark the digging area for the first step.

3 Excavate for the first step, creating a flat bed with a very slight forward slope, no more than ⅛" from back to front. The front of the excavation should be no more than 2" deep. Tamp the soil firmly.

4 For each step, use a chain saw or reciprocating saw to cut a front timber equal to the step width, a back timber 10" shorter, and two side timbers equal to the tread depth.

(continued next page)

5 Arrange the timbers to form the step frame, drill pilot holes, and end-nail the timbers together by driving 12" spikes into the pilot holes.

6 Set the timber frame in position. Use a carpenter's square to make sure the frame is square, and adjust as necessary. Drill two 1" pilot holes in the front timber and the back timber, 1 ft. from the ends, using a spade bit and bit extension.

7 Anchor the steps to the ground by driving a 2½-ft. length of ¾" pipe through each pilot hole until the pipe is flush with the timber. When pipes are driven, make sure the frame is level from side to side and has the proper forward pitch. Excavate for the next step, making sure the bottom of the excavation is even with top edge of the installed timbers.

Drive pipes here

8 Build another step frame and position it in the excavation so the front timber is directly over the rear timber on the first frame. Drill pilot holes, then nail the steps together with three 12" spikes. Drill pilot holes for two pipes, then drive two pipes through only the back timber to anchor the second frame.

9 Continue digging and installing the remaining frames until the steps reach full height. The back of the last step should be at ground level.

10 Staple plastic over the timbers to protect them from wet concrete. Cut away the plastic so it does not overhang into the frame opening.

11 Pour a 2" layer of compactible gravel into each frame as a subbase, and use a 2 × 4 to tamp it down.

12 Mix concrete in a wheelbarrow, adding just enough water so the concrete holds its shape when sliced with a trowel (page 42). NOTE: To save time and labor, you can have ready-mix concrete delivered to the site. Many ready-mix companies will deliver concrete in amounts as small as ⅓ cu. yd. (enough for three steps of the type shown here).

13 Shovel concrete into the bottom frame, flush with the top of the timbers. Work the concrete lightly with a garden rake to help remove air bubbles, but do not overwork the concrete.

(continued next page)

14 Smooth (screed) the concrete by dragging a 2 × 4 across the top of the frame. If necessary, add concrete to low areas and screed again until the surface is smooth and free of low spots.

15 While the concrete is still wet, seed it by scattering mixed gravel onto the surface. Sand-and-gravel suppliers and garden centers sell colorful gravel designed for seeding. For best results, select a mixture with stones no larger than ½" in diameter.

16 Press the seeded gravel into the surface of the concrete, using a float, until the tops of the stones are flush with the surface of the concrete. Remove any concrete that spills over the edges of the frame, using a trowel.

17 Pour concrete into remaining steps, screeding and seeding each step before moving on to the next. Remember to let any bleed water evaporate before seeding (page 49). For a neat appearance, use an edging tool (inset) to shape seams between the timbers and the concrete as you complete each step.

18 Let any bleed water (page 49) disappear. This may take from 30 minutes to several hours, depending on weather conditions. Use a float to smooth out any high or low spots in each step. NOTE: Overfloating (page 49) can force gravel too far into the concrete. Let the concrete dry for about an hour.

19 Apply a fine mist of water to the surface, then scrub it with a stiff brush to expose the seeded gravel.

VARIATION: To save time and money, skip the seeding procedure. Work the concrete, then drag a push broom across it (page 52). To achieve a finer texture and a more weather-resistant surface, wait until the concrete is firm to the touch before using the broom technique.

20 Remove the plastic and cover the concrete with burlap. Allow concrete to cure for a week, spraying it occasionally with water to ensure even curing. NOTE: Concrete can be cleaned from timbers using a 5 percent solution of muriatic acid and water, but the solution may change the color of the timbers.

Landing depth
minimum 12"

Riser height

Overall rise

6" - 8"

Tread dep

10" - 12

Overall run

New concrete steps give a fresh, clean appearance to your house. And if your old steps are unstable, replacing them with concrete steps that have a non-skid surface will create a safer living environment.

Building Concrete Steps

Designing steps requires some calculations and some trial and error. As long as the design meets safety guidelines, you can adjust elements such as the landing depth and the dimensions of the steps. Sketching your plan on paper will make the job easier.

Before demolishing your old steps, measure them to see if they meet safety guidelines. If so, you can use them as a reference for your new steps. If not, start from scratch so your new steps do not repeat any design errors. Consult the section on pouring concrete (pages 46 to 47) for a list of concrete-pouring tools and materials.

For steps with more than two risers, you'll need to install a handrail (page 33). Ask a building inspector about other requirements.

Everything You Need:

Tools: Tape measure, sledge hammer, shovel, drill, reciprocating saw, level, mason's string, hand tamper, mallet, concrete mixing tools, jig saw, clamps, ruler or framing square, float, step edger, broom,

Materials: 2 × 4 lumber, steel rebar grid, wire, bolsters, construction adhesive, compactible gravel, fill material, exterior-grade ¾" plywood, 2" deck screws, isolation board, #3 rebar, stakes, latex caulk, vegetable oil or commercial release agent.

How to Design Steps

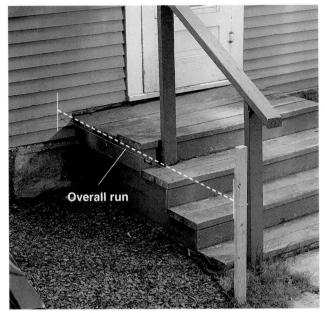

1 Attach a mason's string to the house foundation, 1" below the bottom of the door threshold. Drive a stake where you want the base of the bottom step to fall. Attach the other end of the string to the stake and use a line level to level it. Measure the length of the string—this distance is the overall depth, or *run*, of the steps.

2 Measure down from the string to the bottom of the stake to determine the overall height, or *rise*, of the steps. Divide the overall rise by the estimated number of steps. The rise of each step should be between 6" and 8". For example, if the overall rise is 21" and you plan to build three steps, the rise of each step would be 7" (21 divided by 3), which falls within the recommended safety range for riser height.

3 Measure the width of your door and add at least 12"; this number is the minimum depth you should plan for the landing area of the steps. The landing depth plus the depth of each step should fit within the overall run of the steps. If necessary, you can increase the overall run by moving the stake at the planned base of the steps away from the house, or by increasing the depth of the landing.

4 Sketch a detailed plan for the steps, keeping these guidelines in mind: each step should be 10" to 12" deep, with a riser height between 6" and 8", and the landing should be at least 12" deeper than the swing radius (width) of your door. Adjust the parts of the steps as needed, but stay within the given ranges. Creating a final sketch will take time, but it is worth doing carefully.

How to Build Concrete Steps

1 Remove or demolish existing steps; if the old steps are concrete, set aside the rubble to use as fill material for the new steps. Wear protective gear, including eye protection and gloves, when demolishing concrete.

2 Dig 12"-wide trenches to the required depth (pages 56 to 57). Locate the trenches perpendicular to the foundation, spaced so the footings will extend 3" wider than the outside edges of the steps. Install steel rebar grids (page 59) for reinforcement. Affix isolation boards to the foundation wall inside each trench, using a few dabs of construction adhesive (page 58).

3 Mix the concrete and pour the footings. Level and smooth the concrete with a screed board (page 48). You do not need to float the surface afterwards.

4 When bleed water disappears (page 49), insert 12" sections of rebar 6" into the concrete, spaced at 12" intervals and centered side to side. Leave 1 ft. of clear space at each end.

5 Let the footings cure for two days, then excavate the area between them to 4" deep. Pour in a 5"-thick layer of compactible gravel subbase and tamp until it is level with the footings.

Make slopes ⅛" per foot

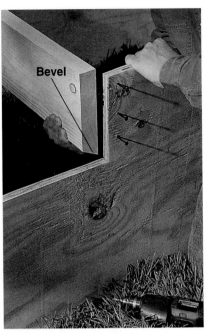

Bevel

6 Transfer the measurements for the side forms from your working sketch onto ¾" exterior-grade plywood. Cut out the forms along the cutting lines, using a jig saw. Save time by clamping two pieces of plywood together and cutting both side forms at the same time. Add a ⅛" per foot back-to-front slope to the landing part of the form.

7 Cut form boards for the risers to fit between the side forms. Bevel the bottom edges of the boards when cutting to create clearance for the float at the back edges of the steps. Attach the riser forms to the side forms with 2" deck screws.

Cleats

Riser support

8 Cut a 2 × 4 to make a center support for the riser forms. Use 2" deck screws to attach 2 × 4 cleats to the riser forms, then attach the support to the cleats. Check to make sure all corners are square.

9 Cut an isolation board (page 37) and glue it to the house foundation at the back of the project area. Set the form onto the footings, flush against the isolation board. Add 2 × 4 bracing arms to the sides of the form, attaching them to cleats on the sides and to stakes driven into the ground.

(continued next page)

10 Fill the form with clean fill (broken concrete or rubble). Stack the fill carefully, keeping it 6" away from the sides, back, and top edges of the form. Shovel smaller fragments onto the pile to fill the void areas.

11 Lay pieces of #3 metal rebar on top of the fill at 12" intervals, and attach them to bolsters with wire to keep them from moving when the concrete is poured. Keep rebar at least 2" below the top of the forms. Mist the forms and the rubble.

12 Coat the forms with vegetable oil or a commercial release agent, then mist them with water so concrete won't stick to the forms. Mix concrete and pour steps one at a time, beginning at the bottom. Settle and smooth the concrete with a screed board (pages 48 to 49). Press a piece of #3 rebar 1" down into the "nose" of each tread for reinforcement.

13 Float the steps, working the front edge of the float underneath the beveled edge at the bottom of each riser form.

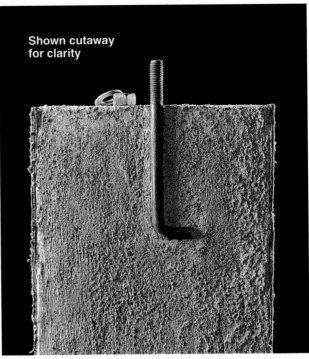

14 Pour concrete into the forms for the remaining steps and the landing. Press rebar into the nose of each step. Keep an eye on the poured concrete as you work, and stop to float any concrete as soon as the bleed water disappears (page 49).

OPTION: For railings with mounting plates that attach to sunken J-bolts, install the bolts before the concrete sets (page 33). Otherwise, choose railings with surface-mounted hardware (see step 16) that can be attached after the steps are completed.

Shown cutaway for clarity

Mounting plate

15 Once the concrete sets, shape the steps and landing with a step edger. Float the surface (page 49). Sweep with a stiff-bristled broom for maximum traction.

16 Remove the forms as soon as the surface is firm to the touch, usually within several hours. Smooth rough edges with a float. Add concrete to fill any holes. If forms are removed later, more patching may be required (pages 247 to 251). Backfill the area around the base of the steps, and seal the concrete (pages 54 to 55). Install a railing.

Pre-cast concrete step forms make it easy to build a durable outdoor staircase. By overlapping the forms in varying arrangements, you can shape a staircase with curves, angles, and even spirals. Lay two forms side-by-side to create larger steps.

Building Steps with Pre-cast Forms

Pre-cast concrete step forms are ideal for building attractive steps without having to build wood forms and pour the concrete yourself. In a few hours, you can excavate, lay pre-cast forms, and pour in concrete. Or, pour a sand bed inside the forms and fill them with brick pavers (above).

Many manufacturers sell pavers that are sized to fit inside the forms they make. Decide how many forms you'll need for the steps you plan to build and the paver pattern you wish to use, then consult the manufacturer's specifications to determine the number of pavers required.

To plan the layout for this project, follow steps 1 to 4 on page 124. You can adjust the amount of overlap for each step to fit the dimensions of your site or to create a desired appearance.

Everything You Need:

Tools: Mason's string, drill, level, shovel, rake, hand tamper, tape measure, rubber mallet, broom.

Materials: Straight 2 x 4 board, stakes, screws, concrete step forms, pavers, compactible gravel, sand.

How to Build Steps with Pre-cast Forms

1 Mark the outline of your steps with stakes and string, then excavate for the first step. Dig a hole 6" deeper than the height of the step and 4" wider and longer than the step on all sides.

2 Fill the hole with compactible gravel. Rake the gravel to create a slight downward slope (⅛" per foot) from back to front, for drainage. Tamp it well with a hand tamper, then set the first form in place. Use a level to make sure the form is level from side to side and has the proper slope from back to front.

3 Add a layer of gravel inside the form and tamp it well. The distance between the gravel and the top of the form should equal the thickness of a paver plus 1". Next, add a 1"-thick layer of sand over the gravel. Use a 2 × 4 set across the form to measure as you go.

4 Lay the pavers in the form in the desired pattern, keeping them level with the top of the form. Adjust as needed, using a rubber mallet or by adding sand underneath. Use a broom to spread sand over the pavers to fill the joints (steps 29 to 30, page 153).

5 Excavate for the next step, accounting for the overlap and a 4" space behind and at the sides for gravel. Fill and tamp the gravel so the front is level with the top of the first step. Repeat steps 2 to 4. When all steps are installed, backfill with dirt along the sides.

Other Step Designs

Wood step frames can be built to create a stairway of any shape, such as the gently curving stairway shown here. Other variations you can try are shown on the opposite page.

Concrete and stone combine to form steps that are elegant and relatively inexpensive.

Brick steps create a formal look that contrasts nicely with an informal riot of flowers

Wood-and-paver steps complement the colorful border that surrounds them. These curving steps echo the informal tone of the rest of the landscape.

Fieldstone is the perfect material when you want to maintain a site's rustic appearance.

This patio replaced a crumbling slab that had become an eyesore. This outdoor room is designed to accommodate more than one activity at a time.

Landings, Patios & Driveways

The techniques for paving horizontal surfaces with masonry share similarities, no matter if the surface is a small entrance landing or an expansive driveway. All these projects will go more smoothly if you plan carefully, reserve an adequate amount of time, and recruit plenty of help. In a few hours, you can resurface a deteriorating concrete landing with fresh mortar and brick pavers. The result is a dressed-up entryway that looks like the work of a professional. Pouring a concrete patio is a 1- to 2-day project that's best handled with one or two helpers. To layout, excavate, and pour a driveway slab, reserve at least a weekend. It's best to have 4 to 5 helpers for the pour.

Tips for Planning:

- Where possible, plan border plantings or other decorative elements to help soften the transition between masonry surfaces and grassy areas.

- Incorporate fences, trellises, or other backyard building structures to enclose an outdoor "room," especially if you have nearby neighbors.

- Create a gentle slope away from your house (⅛" per foot is plenty).

- Design a patio to be roomy: allow at least 20 sq. ft. of patio space for each regular user.

- Lay newspapers or blankets in the proposed building area to help you visualize shapes and sizes in relation to other landscape elements.

Design Tips for Landings, Patios & Driveways

Maintain plenty of clearance between the top of a landing or patio and the door threshold. The top of the landing should be at least 2" below the house sill or threshold so the concrete has room to move without causing damage in the event of frost heave.

Integrate landscaping into a patio design. The exposed-aggregate surface on this patio flows into the texture of the adjoining greenery and rock garden.

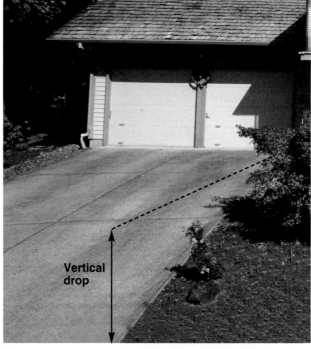

Vertical drop

Incorporate steps or retaining walls into a patio. Originally, the yard in the photo above sloped steeply away from the house. By constructing a retaining wall and integrating steps into the wall, the designer of this masonry project was able to build a patio on what was previously a sharply sloped area.

When planning a driveway pour, use mason's string or a water level (page 177) to find the vertical drop from the garage to the curb. Divide the total drop by the distance in yards to determine the amount of drop per yard. Set stakes along the length of the site to mark positions for the forms.

Variations for Building with Brick Pavers

Basketweave

Herringbone

Consider pattern variations. In addition to the basic running bond and jack-on-jack patterns (page 64), there are many ways to lay pavers for a more decorative effect. The basketweave and herringbone patterns (above) are two common styles. When considering pattern variations, take into account the amount of cutting that is required by some patterns. Generally, diagonal patterns like the herringbone will require cut pavers all the way around the border.

Stand pavers on end (known as *soldier* style) to create a deep border for paving projects. Using soldier-style border pavers is especially effective when you are laying pavers over an existing concrete slab, because the border will hide the exposed edges of the concrete (page 114).

Set pavers into sand for backyard landscaping projects, such as patios and garden walkways. Using sand-set pavers is a quick, easy method for creating masonry projects, but be prepared to re-set pavers occasionally, especially in colder climates, where frost heave may cause a sand-set surface to buckle.

Pour a concrete slab with the surface about 2" below grade to create a solid, permanent foundation for pavers that are bonded together with mortar. Mortared pavers and a sturdy foundation are desirable for paver projects that will experience high traffic, where soil and subsoil below the project are unstable, or in areas where extensive freezing and thawing occur.

Brick pavers and standard building bricks can be used together to create a landing area and planter (pages 230 to 231). Because neither the planter nor the landing is constructed with frost footings, the two must not be attached to one another, so they can move independently without cracking.

Laying a Brick-paver Landing

The entry area is the first detail that visitors to your home will notice. Create a memorable impression by building a brick-paver step landing that gives any house a more formal appearance. Add a special touch to the landing by building a permanent planter next to it (page 230 to 231), using matching brick.

In many cases, a paver landing like the one shown here can be built directly over an existing sidewalk. Make sure the sidewalk is structurally sound and free from major cracks. If adding an adjoining structure, like a planter, create a sepa-

rate building base and be sure to include isolation joints (page 37) so the structure is not connected to the landing area or to the house.

Everything You Need:

Tools: Drill, level, masonry hoe, rubber mallet, mortar bag, jointing tool, mason's trowel.

Materials: Isolation board, type S mortar, pavers, plastic sheeting.

How to Build a Brick-paver Step Landing

Isolation board

1 Dry-lay the pavers onto the concrete surface and experiment with the arrangement to create a layout that uses whole bricks, if possible. Mark outlines for the layout onto the concrete. Attach an isolation board (page 37) to prevent the mortar from bonding with the foundation. Mix a batch of mortar (pages 28 to 31), and dampen the concrete slightly.

2 Lay a bed of mortar for three or four border pavers, starting at one end or corner. Level off the bed to about ½" in depth with the trowel.

3 Begin laying the border pavers, buttering an end of each paver with mortar as you would a brick (page 72). Set pavers into the mortar bed, pressing them down so the bed is ⅜" thick. Cut off excess mortar from the tops and sides of the pavers. Use a level to make sure the pavers are even across the tops, and check mortar joints to confirm that they are uniform in thickness.

4 Finish the border section next to the foundation, checking with a level to make sure the row is even in height. Trim off any excess mortar, then fill in the third border section, leaving the front edge of the project open to provide easier access for laying the interior *field* pavers.

5 Apply a ½"-thick bed of mortar between the border pavers in the work area closest to the foundation. Because mortar is easier to work with when fresh, mix and apply the mortar in small sections (no more than 4 sq. ft.).

6 Begin setting pavers in the field area, without buttering the edges. Check the alignment with a straightedge. Adjust paver height as needed, making sure joints are uniform in width. NOTE: Pavers often are cast with spacing flanges on the sides, but these are for sand-set projects. Use a spacing guide, like a dowel, when setting pavers in mortar.

7 Fill in the rest of the pavers to complete the pattern in the field area, applying mortar beds in small sections. Add the final border section. Every 30 minutes add mortar to joints between pavers until it is even with the tops. TIP: To minimize mess when adding mortar, use a mortar bag to deliver the mortar into the joints.

8 Smooth and shape the mortar joints with a jointing tool. Tool the full-width "running" joints first, then tool the joints at the ends of the pavers. Let the mortar dry for a few hours, then remove any residue by scrubbing the pavers with a coarse rag and water. Cover the walkway with plastic and let the mortar cure for at least two days. Remove plastic, but do not walk on the pavers for at least one week.

Laying a Brick-paver Patio

Laying a patio with brick pavers and sand is simple and results in a patio that is attractive and functional. A patio functions best when it is as large as a standard room, 100 square feet or more. An array of patio paver types is available to match your home and complement landscape elements (pages 64 to 65).

Everything You Need:

Tools: Tape measure, level, mason's string, shovel, line level, rake, hand tamper, power tamper, rubber mallet, chisel, maul, circular saw, masonry blade.

Materials: Stakes, compactible gravel, rigid plastic edging, galvanized spikes, landscape fabric, sand, pavers, 1"-thick pipes.

How to Build a Brick-paver Patio

1 To find exact patio measurements and reduce the number of cut bricks needed, test-fit perpendicular rows of brick pavers on a flat surface. Lay two rows to reach the rough length and width of your patio, then measure the rows to find the exact size.

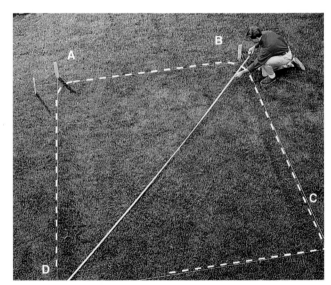

2 With stakes and mason's strings, plot a rectangle that matches the dimensions of your patio, using the 3-4-5 triangle method (page 178). Make sure that the rectangle is square: the diagonals (A to C and B to D) must have the same measurement. If not, adjust the stakes until the diagonals are equal. The strings will serve as a reference for excavating the patio site.

146

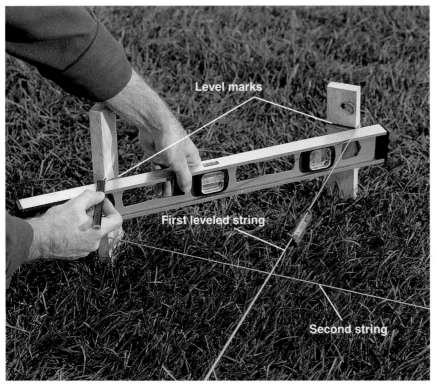

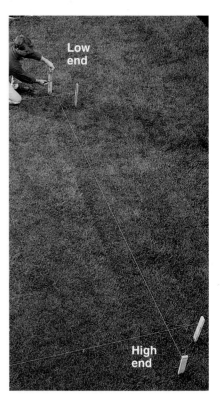

3 Using a line level as a guide, adjust one of the strings until it is level. When the string is level, mark its height on the stakes at each end. To adjust each remaining string so it is level and even with the first string, use a level as a guide for marking adjacent stakes, then adjust the strings to the reference marks. Use a line level to make sure that all strings are level.

4 To ensure proper drainage, a patio should slope ⅛" per foot away from the house. Measure from the high end to the low end (in feet) and multiply the number by ⅛. Measure down from the level marks on the low-end stakes, and mark the drop distance.

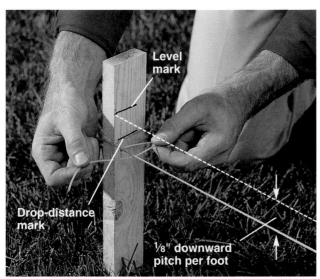

5 Lower the strings at the low-end stakes so the strings are even with the drop distance marks. Keep all strings in place as a guide while excavating and installing edging.

6 Remove all sod inside the strings and 6" beyond the edges of the planned patio. NOTE: If your patio will have rounded corners, use a garden hose or rope to outline the excavation.

(continued next page)

How to Build a Brick-paver Patio (continued)

7 Starting at the outside edge, excavate the patio site so it is at least 5" deeper than the thickness of the pavers. For example, if your pavers are 1¾" thick, excavate to a depth of 6¾". Follow the slope of the side strings, and periodically use a long 2 × 4 to check the bottom of the excavation site for high and low spots.

8 Pour compactible gravel over the patio site, then rake it into a smooth layer at least 4" deep. The thickness of the subbase layer may vary to compensate for unevenness in the excavation. Use a long 2 × 4 to check the surface of the subbase for high and low spots, and add or remove compactible gravel as needed.

9 Pack the subbase, using a power tamper, until the surface is firm and flat. Check the slope of the subbase by measuring down from the side strings (see step 12). The space between the strings and the subbase should be equal at all points.

10 Cut strips of landscape fabric and lay them over the subbase to contain the gravel and prevent weeds from growing up through the patio. Make sure the strips overlap by at least 6".

11 Install rigid plastic edging around the edges of the patio below the reference strings. Anchor the edging by driving galvanized spikes through the predrilled holes and into the subbase. To allow for possible adjustments, drive only enough spikes to keep the edging in place.

12 Check the slope by measuring from the string to the top of the edging at several points. The measurement should be the same at each point. If not, adjust the edging by adding or removing sub-base material under the landscape fabric until the edging follows the slope of the strings.

13 For curves and rounded patio corners, use rigid plastic edging with notches on the outside flange. It may be necessary to anchor each section of edging with spikes to hold curved edging in place.

14 Remove the reference strings, then set 1"-thick pipes or wood strips across the patio area, spaced every 6 ft., to serve as depth spacers for laying the sand base.

(continued next page)

15 Lay a 1"-thick layer of sand over the landscape fabric and smooth it out with a garden rake. Sand should just cover the tops of the depth spacers.

16 Water the sand thoroughly, and pack it lightly with a hand tamper.

17 Screed the sand to an even layer by resting a long 2 × 4 on the spacers embedded in the sand and drawing the 2 × 4 across the spacers, using a sawing motion. Add extra sand to fill footprints and low areas, then water, tamp, and screed the sand again until it is smooth and firmly packed.

18 Remove the embedded spacers along the sides of the patio base, then fill the grooves with sand and pat them smooth with the hand tamper.

19 Lay the first border paver in one corner of the patio. Make sure the paver rests firmly against the rigid plastic edging.

20 Lay the next border paver so it is roughly ⅛" from previous paver. Set the pavers by tapping them into the sand with a rubber mallet. Use the depth of the first paver as a guide for setting the remaining pavers.

21 Working outward from the corner, install 2-ft.-wide sections of border pavers and interior pavers, following the desired pattern. Keep the joints between pavers very tight. Set each paver by tapping it with the mallet.

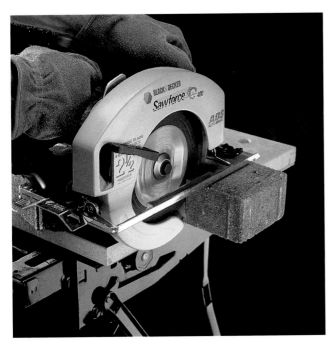

22 Depending on the pattern you choose, you may need to split some pavers. Score the pavers first, using a chisel and maul or a circular saw with a masonry blade (pages 70 to 71). Make the final cuts with a chisel and maul. Wear eye protection and work gloves when using cutting tools.

23 After each section of pavers is set, use a straightedge to make sure the pavers are flat Make adjustments by tapping high pavers deeper into the sand or by removing low pavers and adding a thin layer of extra sand underneath them.

(continued next page)

24 Remove the remaining spacers when the installed surface gets near to them. Fill the gaps left by the spacers with loose sand, and pat the surface smooth with a hand tamper (inset).

25 Continue installing 2-ft.-wide sections of border pavers and interior pavers. As you approach the opposite side of the patio, reposition the rigid plastic edging, if necessary, so full-sized pavers will fit without cutting.

26 At rounded corners and curves, install border pavers in a fan pattern with even gaps between the pavers. Gentle curves may accommodate full-sized border pavers, but for sharper bends you may need to mark and trim wedge-shaped border pavers to make them fit.

27 Lay the remaining interior pavers. Where partial pavers are needed, hold a paver over the gap, and mark the cut with a pencil and straightedge. Cut pavers with a circular saw and masonry blade (step 22, page 151). After all pavers are installed, drive in the remaining edging spikes and pack soil behind the edging.

28 Use a long, straight 2 × 4 to make sure the entire patio is flat. Adjust high pavers by tapping them deeper into the sand. Remove low pavers and add a thin layer of extra sand underneath. After adjusting uneven pavers, use line blocks and mason's string to check that rows are straight.

29 Spread a ½" layer of sand over the patio. Use a power tamper to compress the entire patio and pack sand into the joints.

30 Sweep up the loose sand, then soak the patio area thoroughly to settle the sand in the joints. Let the surface dry completely. If necessary, repeat step 29 until the gaps between pavers are packed tightly with sand.

Dry-mortar option: For a finished masonry look, install pavers with ⅜" gaps. Fill the gaps with a dry mixture made from 4 parts sand and 1 part dry mortar. After spreading the dry mixture and tamping the patio, sprinkle the surface with water. Finish the wet mortar joints with a jointing tool. After mortar hardens, scrub the pavers with water and a coarse rag.

Building an Exposed-aggregate Patio

An exposed-aggregate patio project relies on basic site-preparation and concrete-pouring techniques, and adds an attractive finish.

Everything You Need:

Tools: Shovel, rope or hose, mason's string, tape measure, hand tamper, level, drill, wheelbarrow, masonry hoe, hammer, screed board, mason's trowel, edger, magnesium float, stiff-bristle brush, hose and spray attachment, paint roller.

Materials: 2½" and 4" deck screws, stakes, compactible gravel, pressure-treated 2 × 4s, reinforcing mesh, bolsters, small aggregate, type N concrete mix, plastic sheeting, exposed-aggregate sealer.

A concrete slab project becomes an attractive patio when divided by wood forms and seeded with stones. The forms replace control joints and a gravel subbase provides stability and drainage. Refer to the section on laying out and excavating your site (pages 36 to 39) before starting your project.

How to Build an Exposed-aggregate Patio

1 Prepare the building site by removing any existing building materials, like sidewalks or landing areas. Consider the design tips on the previous page and throughout this book, and select a design for your concrete patio.

2 Lay out the rough position of the patio using a rope or hose, then mark the exact layout with stakes and mason's strings. Measure the diagonals to make sure the project area is square (page 146). Establish a ⅛" per ft. slope away from the house (pages 36 to 37).

3 Remove sod and excavate the project area to a consistent depth, using mason's strings and a story pole as reference (page 39).

4 Create a subbase for the patio by pouring a 5"-thick layer of compactible gravel, then tamping until it is even and 4" thick.

5 Cut brown pressure-treated 2 × 4 boards to build a permanent form frame that outlines the entire patio site. Lay the boards in place, using the mason's strings as guides. Fasten the ends together with 2½" galvanized deck screws. Temporarily stake the forms at 2-ft. intervals. Set a straight 2 × 4 across the side forms, and set a level on top of the 2 × 4 to check the side forms for level. SAFETY TIP: Wear gloves and a particle mask when cutting pressure-treated lumber.

Half-length form boards

Full-length form board

6 Cut and install pressure-treated 2 × 4s to divide the square into quadrants: cut one piece full length, and attach two one-half length pieces to it with screws driven toenail style. Drive 4" deck screws partway into the forms every 12" at inside locations. The portions that stick out will act as tie rods between the poured concrete and the permanent forms. TIP: Protect the tops of the permanent forms by covering them with masking tape.

(continued next page)

7 Cut reinforcing wire mesh to fit inside each quadrant, leaving 1" clearance on all sides (pages 37 and 41). Mix concrete and pour the quadrants one at a time, starting with the one located farthest from the concrete source (pages 42 to 47). Use a masonry hoe to spread the concrete evenly in the forms.

8 Settle the concrete by sliding a spade along the inside edges of the forms and rapping the outer edges with a hammer. Smooth off the concrete using a straight 2 × 4 as a screed board (page 48). Let any bleed water disappear before continuing (page 49).

9 After screeding the surface, cover the concrete with a full layer of aggregate *seeds*. Use a magnesium float to embed the aggregate completely into the concrete (page 53).

10 Tool the edges of the quadrant with an edger, then use a float to smooth any marks left behind. TIP: If you plan to pour more quadrants immediately, cover the seeded concrete with plastic so it does not set up too quickly.

11 Pour the remaining quadrants, repeating steps 7 to 10. Check poured quadrants periodically; uncover the quadrants once any bleed water has evaporated (page 49).

12 Once any bleed water has evaporated, mist the surface with water and scrub the surface with a stiff-bristled brush. Remove the protective tape from the forms, then re-cover the quadrants with plastic and let the concrete cure for a week (page 52).

13 After the concrete has cured, rinse and scrub the aggregate again to clean off any remaining residue. TIP: Use diluted muriatic acid to wash off stubborn concrete residue. Read manufacturer's instructions for mixing ratios and safety precautions.

14 Once the patio has cured for three weeks, seal the surface with exposed-aggregate sealer. Reapply sealer annually, following manufacturer's recommendations.

Patio tile can turn a drab concrete slab into a charming outdoor living area. To create this tiled project, we first poured a new concrete subbase over an existing concrete patio (inset).

New subbase

Old patio

Finishing a Patio with Tile

If you have ever laid ceramic or vinyl tile inside your house, you already have valuable experience that will help you lay patio tile.

The primary differences between interior and exterior tile are in the thickness of the tiles and the water-absorption rates. The project layout and application techniques are quite similar. For any type of tiling project, preparing or creating a suitable subbase for the tiles can become a fairly intensive project. A sturdy subbase is critical.

Patio tile is most frequently applied over a concrete subbase—either an existing concrete patio, or a new concrete slab. A third option, which we show you on the following pages, is to pour a new tile subbase over an existing concrete patio. This option involves far less work and expense than removing an old patio and pouring a new slab. And it ensures that your new tiled patio will not develop the same problems that may be present in the existing concrete surface.

See the photographs at the top of page 160 to help you determine the best method for preparing an existing concrete patio for tile.

If you do not have a concrete slab in the project area already, you will need to pour one (pages 34 to 51).

The patio tiling project shown here is divided into two separate projects: pouring a new subbase and installing patio tile. If your existing patio is in good condition, you do not need to pour a new subbase.

When selecting tiles for your patio, make sure the product you purchase is exterior tile, which is designed to withstand freezing and thawing better than interior tile. Try to select colors and textures that match or complement other parts of your house and yard. If your project requires extensive tile cutting, rent a wet saw or arrange to have the tiles cut to size at the supply center.

Exterior tile products for patios are denser and thicker than interior tile. Common types include shell-stone tile, ceramic patio tile, and quarry tile. The most common size is 12" × 12", but you also can purchase precut designer tiles that are assembled into elaborate patterns and designs.

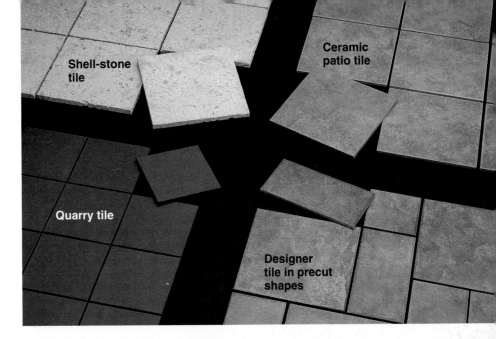

Tools for working with exterior tile include: a wet saw for cutting large amounts of tile (usually a rental item), a square-notched trowel for spreading tile adhesive (consult the tile manufacturer's instructions regarding the proper notch size), a grout float for spreading grout into joints between tiles, a sponge for wiping up excess grout, tile nippers for making curved or angled cuts in tiles, tile spacers to set standard joints between tiles, and a rubber mallet for setting tiles into adhesive.

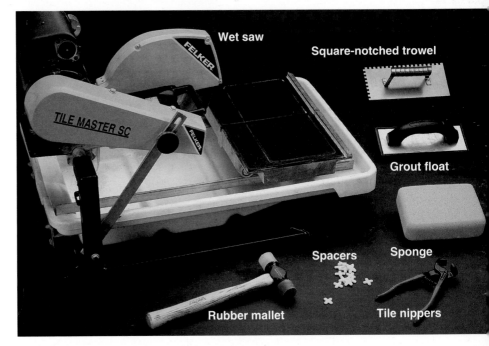

Materials for installing patio tile include: exterior tile grout (tinted or untinted), acrylic grout sealer, metal stucco lath as reinforcement for concrete slab, latex caulk for filling tile joints over control joints, caulk backer rod to keep grout out of control joints during grout application, latex-fortified grout additive, tile sealer, floor-mix concrete for building a tile subbase, tile adhesive (dry-set mortar), and a mortar bag for filling joints with grout (optional).

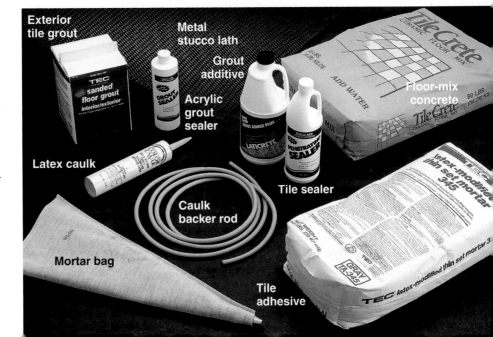

Tips for Evaluating Concrete Surfaces

A good surface is free from any major cracks or badly flaking concrete (called spalling). You can apply patio tile directly over a concrete surface that is in good condition if it has control joints (see below).

A fair surface may exhibit minor cracking and spalling, but has no major cracks or badly deteriorated spots. Install a new concrete subbase over a surface in fair condition before laying patio tile.

A poor surface contains deep or large cracks, broken, sunken or heaved concrete, or extensive spalling. If you have this kind of surface, remove the concrete completely and replace it with a new concrete slab before you lay patio tile.

Tips for Cutting Control Joints in a Concrete Patio

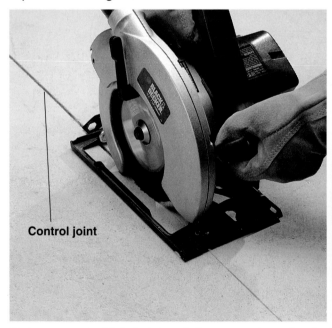

Control joint

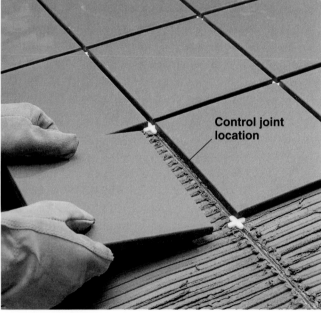

Control joint location

Cut new control joints into existing concrete patios that are in good condition (see above) but do not have enough control joints. Control joints will allow inevitable cracking to occur in locations that don't weaken the concrete or detract from its appearance. They should be cut every 5 or 6 ft. in a patio. Plan the control joints so they will be below tile joints once the tile layout is established. Use a circular saw with a masonry blade set to ⅜" depth to cut control joints. Cover the saw base with duct tape to prevent scratching.

How to Install a Subbase for Patio Tile

Everything You Need:

Tools: Basic hand tools, shovel, maul, straight-edge, aviation snips, masonry hoe, mortar box, hand tamper, magnesium float, concrete edger, utility knife, margin trowel.

Materials: 30# building paper, plastic sheeting, 2 × 4 and 2 × 2 lumber, 2½" and 3" deck screws, ⅜" stucco lath, roofing cement.

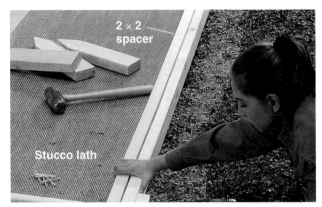

1 Dig a trench at least 6" wide, and no more than 4" deep, around the patio to create room for 2 × 4 forms. Clean dirt and debris from the exposed sides of the patio. Cut and fit 2 × 4 frames around the patio, joining the ends with 3" deck screws. Cut wood stakes from 2 × 4s and drive them next to the forms, at 2-ft. intervals.

2 Adjust the form height: set stucco lath on the surface, then set a 2 × 2 spacer on top of the lath (their combined thickness equals the thickness of the subbase). Adjust the form boards so the tops are level with the 2 × 2, and screw the stakes to the forms with 2½" deck screws.

3 Remove the 2 × 2 spacers and stucco lath, then lay strips of 30# building paper over the patio surface, overlapping seams by 6", to create a *bond-breaker* for the new surface. Crease the building paper at the edges and corners, making sure the paper extends past the tops of the forms. Make a small cut in the paper at each corner for easier folding.

4 Lay strips of stucco lath over the building-paper bond-breaker, overlapping seams by 1". Keep the lath 1" away from forms and the wall. Use aviation snips to cut the stucco lath (wear heavy gloves when handling metal).

(continued next page)

How to Install a Subbase for Patio Tile (continued)

5 Build temporary 2 × 2 forms to divide the project into working sections and provide rests for the screed board used to level and smooth the fresh concrete. Make the sections narrow enough that you can reach across the entire section (3-ft. to 4-ft. sections are comfortable for most people). Screw the ends of the 2 × 2s to the form boards so the tops are level.

6 Mix dry floor-mix concrete with water in a mortar box, blending with a masonry hoe, according to the manufacturer's directions, or use a power mixer (page 44).

NOTE: The mixture should be very dry when prepared so it can be pressed down into the voids in the stucco lath with a tamper.

7 Fill one working section with floor-mix concrete, up to the tops of the forms. Tamp the concrete thoroughly with a lightweight tamper to help force it into the voids in the lath and into corners. The lightweight tamper shown above is made from a 12" × 12" piece of ¾" plywood, with a 2 × 4 handle attached.

162

8 Level off the surface of the concrete by dragging a straight 2 × 4 screed board across the top, with the ends riding on the forms. Move the 2 × 4 in a sawing motion as you progress, creating a level surface and filling any voids in the concrete. If voids or hollows remain, add more concrete and smooth it off.

9 Use a magnesium float to smooth the surface of the concrete. Applying very light pressure, move the float back and forth in an arching motion, tipping the lead edge up slightly to avoid gouging the surface.

10 Pour and smooth out the next working section, repeating steps 7 to 9. After floating this section, remove the 2 × 2 temporary form between the two sections. Fill the void left behind with fresh concrete. Float the fresh concrete with the magnesium float until the concrete is smooth and level and blends into the working section on each side. Pour and finish the remaining working sections one at a time, using the same techniques.

(continued next page)

How to Install a Subbase for Patio Tile (continued)

11 Let the concrete dry until pressing the surface with your finger does not leave a mark. Cut contours around all edges of the subbase with a concrete edger. Tip the lead edge of the edger up slightly to avoid gouging the surface. Smooth out any marks left by the edger using a float.

12 Cover the concrete with sheets of plastic, and cure for at least three days (see manufacturer's directions for recommended curing time). Weight down the edges of the sheeting. After curing is compete, remove the plastic and disassemble and remove the forms.

13 Trim off the building paper around the sides of the patio using a utility knife. Apply roofing cement to three sides of the patio, using a trowel or putty knife to fill and seal the seam between the old and new surfaces. To provide drainage for moisture between layers, do not seal the lowest side of the patio. After the roofing cement dries, shovel dirt or ground cover back into the trench around the patio.

Laying Patio Tile

With any tiling project, the most important part of the job is creating and marking the layout lines and pattern for the tile. The best way to do this is to perform a dry run using the tiles you will install. Try to find a layout that requires the least possible amount of cutting.

Once you have established an efficient layout plan, carefully mark square reference lines in the project area. Creating a professional-looking tiled patio requires that you follow the lines and use sound installation techniques.

Some patio tile is fashioned with small ridges on the edges that automatically establish the spacing between tiles. But more often, you will need to insert plastic spacers between tiles as you work. The spacers should be removed before the tile adhesive dries.

Tiled patios are vulnerable to cracking. Make sure the tile subbase has sufficient control joints to keep cracking in check (page 160). Install tiles so the tile joints align with the control joints. Fill the tile joints over the control joints with flexible latex caulk, rather than grout.

Everything You Need:

Tools: Carpenter's square, straightedge, tape measure, chalk line, tile cutter or wet saw, tile nippers, square-notched trowel, needlenose pliers, rubber mallet, grout float, grout sponge, caulk gun.

Materials: Tile spacers, buckets, paint brush and roller, plastic sheeting, paper towels, dry-set mortar, tile, backer rod, grout, grout additive, latex tile caulk, grout sealer, tile sealer.

How to Lay Patio Tile

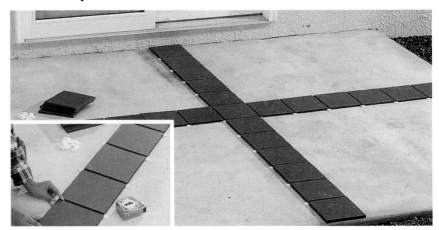

1 Without applying adhesive, dry-lay rows of tile on the surface so they run in each direction, intersecting at the center of the patio. Slip tile spacers between tiles to represent joints (inset). Keep the tiles ¼" to ½" away from the house to allow for expansion. This *dry lay* helps you establish and mark an attractive, efficient layout for the tile.

2 Adjust the tile to create a layout that minimizes tile cutting. Shift the rows of tiles and spacers until the overhang is equal at each end and any cut portions are less than 2" wide.

Snap chalk line for reference

3 Once the layout is set, mark layout lines onto the tiling surface. Mark the surface at the joint between the third and fourth row out from the house, then measure the distance and mark it at several more points along the project area. Snap a chalk line to connect the marks.

(continued next page)

4 Use a carpenter's square and a long, straight board to mark end points for a second reference line perpendicular to the first. Mark the points next to the dry-laid tile so the line falls on a joint location. Remove tools and tiles, and snap a chalk line that connects the points.

5 Lay tiles in one quadrant at a time, beginning with a section next to the house. Start by mixing a batch of dry-set mortar in a bucket, according to the manufacturer's directions. Spread mortar evenly along both legs of one quadrant using a square-notched trowel. Apply enough mortar for four tiles along each leg.

6 Use the edge of the trowel to create furrows in the mortar. Make sure you have applied enough mortar to completely cover the area under the tiles without covering up the reference lines.

7 Set the first tile in the corner of the quadrant where the lines intersect, pressing down lightly and twisting slightly from side to side. Adjust the tile until it is exactly aligned with both reference lines.

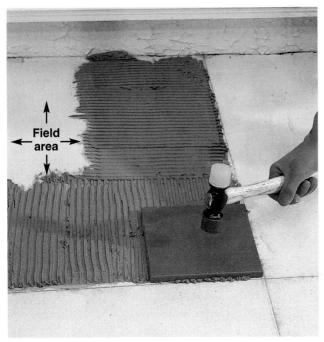

8 Rap the tile gently with a rubber mallet to set it into the mortar. Rap evenly across the entire surface area, being careful not to break the tile or completely displace the mortar beneath the tile. NOTE: Once you start to fill in the *field* area of the quadrant, it is faster to place several tiles at once, then set them all with the mallet at one time.

9 Set plastic spacers at the corner of the tile that faces the working quadrant.

10 Position the next tile into the mortar bed along one arm of the quadrant, making sure the tiles fit neatly against the spacers. Rap the tile with the mallet to set it into the mortar, then position and set the next tile on the other leg of the quadrant. Make certain the tiles align with the reference lines.

11 Fill out the rest of the tile in the mortared area of the quadrant using the spacers to maintain uniform joints between tiles. Wipe off any excess mortar before it dries. NOTE: Plastic spacers are temporary: remove them before the mortar hardens—usually within one hour.

(continued next page)

12 Apply a furrowed layer of mortar to the field area: do not cover more area than you can tile in 15 to 20 minutes. TIP: Start with smaller sections, then increase the size as you get a better idea of your working pace.

13 Set tiles into the field area of the first quadrant, saving any cut tiles for last. Rent a wet saw from your local rental store for cutting tiles, or use a tile cutter. For curved cuts, use tile nippers.

14 Apply mortar and fill in tiles in the next quadrant against the house, using the same techniques used for the first quadrant. Carefully remove plastic spacers with needlenose pliers as you finish each quadrant—do not leave spacers in mortar for more than one hour. Make sure to clean all excess mortar from the tiles before it hardens.

15 Fill in the remaining quadrants. Tɪᴘ: Use a straightedge to check the tile joints occasionally. If you find that any of the joint lines are out of alignment, compensate for the misalignment over several rows of tiles.

16 After all the tiles for the patio are set, check to make sure all spacers are removed and any excess mortar has been cleaned from the tile surfaces. Cover the project area with plastic for three days to allow the mortar to cure properly.

Caulking backer rod

17 After three days, remove the plastic and prepare the tile for grouting (the process of filling the joints between tiles with grout). Create expansion joints on the tiled surface by inserting strips of ¼"-diameter caulking backer rod into the joints between quadrants and over any control joints, to keep grout out of these joints.

(continued next page)

18 Mix a batch of tile grout to the recommended consistency. TIP: Add latex-fortified grout additive so excess grout is easier to remove. Starting in a corner and working out, pour a layer of grout onto an area of the surface that is 25 sq. ft. or less in size. Use a rubber grout float to spread the grout and pack it into the joints between tiles.

19 Use the grout float to scrape off excess grout from the surface of the tile. Scrape diagonally across the joints, holding the float in a near-vertical position. Patio tile will absorb grout quickly and permanently, so it is important to remove all excess grout from the surface before it sets. NOTE: It's a good idea to have helpers when working on large areas.

20 Use a damp sponge to wipe the grout film from the surface of the tile. Rinse the sponge out frequently with cool water, and be careful not to press down so hard around joints that you disturb the grout. Wash grout off of the entire surface.

21 Let the grout dry for about four hours, then poke it with a nail to make sure it has hardened. Use a cloth to buff the surface until any remaining grout film is gone. If buffing does not remove all the film, try using a coarser cloth, such as burlap, or even an abrasive pad to remove stubborn grout film.

22 Remove the caulking backer rod from the tile joints, then fill the joints with caulk that is tinted to match the grout color closely. The caulk will allow for some expansion and contraction of the tiled surface, preventing cracking and buckling.

23 Apply grout sealer to the grout lines using a sash brush or small sponge brush. Avoid spilling over onto the tile surface with the grout sealer. Wipe up any spills immediately.

24 After one to three weeks, seal the surface with tile sealer, following the manufacturer's application directions. A paint roller with an extension pole is a good tool for applying tile sealer.

Find the slope of your current driveway by dividing the length in feet (the horizontal distance from the apron to the curb) by the vertical drop (page 141) in inches. This tells you how many inches per foot the new driveway should slope. It's easiest to use a water level (page 177) to measure the vertical drop. Joints cut in the driveway's surface or created with strips of felt placed between sections of the driveway reduce damage from cracking and buckling. A crowned surface encourages water to run off to the sides.

Pouring a Concrete Driveway

Pouring a driveway is a lot like pouring a patio or walk, but on a larger scale. It's particularly useful to divide the driveway into sections that you can pour one at a time. A wood divider (page 174) is removed after each section is firm and repositioned to pour the next section. For driveways wider than 10 ft., a control joint is added down the center to keep cracks from spreading. Driveways up to 10 ft. wide are simplest because you can pour fiber-reinforced concrete directly over the subbase without additional reinforcement. (Check with your building inspector regarding local requirements.) For a larger slab, add metal reinforcement, using the approach used for a walkway (page 107).

Pay attention to drainage conditions when planning your driveway. Soil that drains poorly can damage a slab (pages 26 to 27). If drainage is poor (page 15), line your site with polyethylene

Everything You Need:

Tools: Level, water level, mason's string, screed board, mallet, wheelbarrow, circular saw, drill, broom, coarse brush, hand float, concrete edger and groover, darby, shovel, wheelbarrow, hoe, spade, hammer, trowel, edger, bucket, measuring tape, hand tamper or power tamper.

Materials: Stakes, 2 × 4 and 1 × 2 lumber, crushed stone, fiber-reinforced concrete mix, 4"-wide bituminous felt, 2" deck screws, vegetable oil or commercial release agent, 6 mil plastic sheeting.

sheeting before pouring. It is critical to establish a gradual slope, using the approach shown in the photo above and a crowned surface, so water runs off the driveway. NOTE: It's important to handle bleed water carefully as you pour a driveway. Review the section on bleed water (page 49) before beginning your project.

How to Lay Out a Driveway Slab

Laying Out the Site

A proper layout is key to determining how well your driveway functions. Start by calculating the amount of drop per foot on the site (page 172). You need this number so you can maintain a gradual slope as you excavate. Plan to excavate an area 10" wider than the slab. This allows room for stakes and forms that will hold the concrete in place (pages 38 to 39). How deep you need to dig depends on the thickness of the slab and the subbase, typically 4" each. (Check with your building inspector. Building Codes in some areas call for a 6" slab—in that case, you'll need 2 × 6s instead of 2 × 4s for forms.) Use beveled 12" 1 × 2 stakes and mason's strings to mark the edges of the site. Set the stakes at a consistent height so you can use them to check the depth of the excavated site.

8" (minimum depth)

1 Excavate the site (pages 38 to 39), using stakes and mason's strings to establish the proper slope. You may have to remove the stakes temporarily to smooth the bottom of the site with a 2 × 4 and pack the soil with a tamper.

2 Pour a 4" layer of crushed stone as a subbase. Screed with a long 2 × 4, then tamp the stone. You can make small adjustments to the slope of the site, as required, by adjusting the thickness of the subbase.

3½"

3 Drive stakes at the corners of the site, 3½" in from each side. Connect the stakes on each side with mason's strings. Use a water level (inset, right) to check that the strings are set to the correct slope. Adjust the stakes as necessary.

4 Position 2 × 4 forms inside the strings with the tops level with the strings. Plant stakes every 2 ft. outside the forms, with the tops slightly lower than the tops of the forms. Drive deck screws through the stakes and into the forms. Where forms meet (above), secure them to a single 1 × 4 stake.

(continued next page)

OPTION: Use 1 × 4s to create forms for turns in the driveway. Saw parallel ½"-deep *kerfs* in one side of each board, and bend the boards to form the proper curves. Attach the curved forms inside the stakes. Backfill beneath all of the forms.

5 Construct a divider equal in length to the width of the slab. Set a 1 × 2 on the edge of a 2 × 4; place a ⅝" × 1½" wood spacer midway between them, flush with the edges. Attach the two pieces with 2" deck screws so the screw heads sink below the surface. The curved top of the divider will form the crown of the driveway as you screed.

⅝"
spacer between boards

6 Position the divider roughly 6 ft. from the top of the driveway. Drive screws through the forms and into the divider to hold it in place temporarily. Place a felt isolation strip against the divider. Prop the strip in place temporarily with bricks. NOTE: If your site drains poorly (pages 26 to 27), add a layer of polyethylene over the bottom of the site as a vapor barrier.

7 Coat the dividers and forms with vegetable oil or commercial release agent (page 40) so concrete won't bond to their surfaces as it cures. Mix fiber-reinforced concrete for one section of the slab at a time, using a power mixer, or order concrete from a ready-mix supplier. If you use ready-mix, have helpers on hand so you can pour the concrete as soon as it arrives.

How to Pour a Driveway Slab

1 Pour pods of concrete (pages 46 to 47) into the first section, digging into the concrete with a shovel to eliminate air pockets. Remove the brick props inside the site once there is sufficient concrete in place to prop up the felt strip.

2 Screed the concrete from side to side, using a 2 × 4 resting on the driveway apron and the crowned divider. Raise the leading edge of the board slightly as you move it across the concrete. Add concrete to any low spots. Rescreed if necessary.

3 Float the surface with a darby, then let the surface cure for 2-4 hours, or until it is solid enough to support your weight. NOTE: For a slab wider than 10 ft., cut a control joint down the slab's center line (page 172).

4 Use an edger along the inside of the forms to create smooth edges (page 49). Remove the divider and screw it in place alongside a felt strip to pour the next section. Screw the divider in place and prop it with bricks.

5 Finish the surface as desired as each section hardens (page 52). Cover the sections with polyethylene sheeting, misting daily for two weeks (pages 52 to 53). Remove the forms and seal the concrete (pages 54 to 55).

Cut stone is a top-quality material for building walls, pillars and arches. For retaining walls (shown above) cut stone or interlocking block is laid without mortar (except for the top course) so water doesn't become trapped behind the wall. Free-standing structures are often built with mortar (we include both types in this section). Either method can be used to build walls that will last for generations. Both are described in this section.

Walls, Pillars & Arches

Vertical masonry structures can be as simple or as grand as you chose. Because of the strength and durability of masonry, you are limited only by your imagination, time, and energy. The projects presented here include some of the easiest and most popular—from constructing a concrete block wall with an attractive finish, to building a sturdy retaining wall. Also included are more challenging projects that add a touch of elegance. They include arched brick pillars and a stone wall with a *moon window.* Even these projects are surprisingly easy if you approach them patiently. Of course, you don't have to use the identical materials. You can construct your arch with stone or build a moon window with brick. Before starting, read the sections under Basic Techniques (pages 26 to 97) devoted to the materials you plan to use.

Finished with stucco (pages 220 to 221) and topped with lattice panels (page 184), this concrete block wall forms an attractive divider between a patio and yard.

How to Lay Out a Wall, Pillar, or Arch

1 To get a sense of the size and impact of a wall or other project before you begin construction, plot the borders of the project, using tall stakes or poles, then tie mason's strings marking the projected top of the structure.

2 Hang landscape fabric or sheets of plastic between the stakes and over the top of the string. View the structure from all sides for an indication of how much it will obstruct views and access, and how it will blend with other elements of the landscape.

Working with a Water Level

Water levels take advantage of the fact that water in an open tube will level itself, no matter how many bends and turns the tube has. This makes a water level ideal for working with long structures, around corners, or on sites where a conventional level won't work. Typical commercially available water levels consist of clear plastic tubes that screw onto the ends of a garden hose (right, top). Mark off 1" increments on each tube. Attach the tubes to the ends of a garden hose, then fill the hose until water is visible in both tubes. Working with a helper, hold the tubes at the ends of the site. Adjust the tubes until the water is at the same mark in each tube (right, bottom). Drive stakes or mark off the level points on your structure. OPTION: Pricier water levels contain an electronic gauge that's useful when you need precise readings.

How to Plot a Right Angle

1 The 3-4-5 triangle method is the most effective method of plotting right angles for walls, pillars, and other construction. Begin by staking the outside corner of your walls and stringing a mason's string to mark the outside of one wall.

2 Mark a point 3 ft. out along that wall by planting another stake.

3 Position the end of one tape measure at the outside corner and open it past the 4 ft. mark. Have an assistant position the end of another tape measure at the 3 ft. stake and open it past the 5 ft. mark. Lock the tape measures and adjust them so they intersect at the 4 ft. and 5 ft. marks.

4 Plant a stake at the meeting point, then run mason's strings from this stake to the outside corner. The 3 ft. and 4 ft. mason's strings form a right angle. Extend or shorten the mason's strings, as required, and stake out the exact dimensions of your structure.

How to Plot a Curve

1 Start by plotting a right angle, using the 3-4-5 triangle method (opposite page). Mark the end points for the curve by measuring and planting stakes equidistant from the outside corner.

2 Tie a mason's string to those stakes. Extend each string back to the outside corner, then hold them tight at the point where they meet. Pull this point toward the inside of the angle until the strings are taut. The strings will complete a square.

3 Plant a stake at their meeting point, then tie a piece of mason's string to that stake, just long enough to reach the stakes marking the endpoints of the curve.

4 Pull the string taut, then swing it in an arc between the end points, using spray paint to mark the curve on the ground.

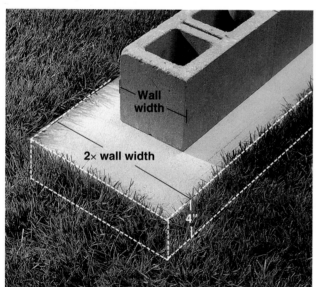

Begin a freestanding block wall project with a properly sized footing (pages 56 to 59).

Building Freestanding Block Walls without Mortar

The project below shows how to lay a block wall without using mortar between blocks. Mortarless walls are built using a running bond pattern (page 65), and are simple to construct. They derive their strength from a coating of surface bonding cement on all exposed surfaces (pages 214 to 215). The cement creates a bond between blocks that is strong enough to support even very long walls. The coating is similar in appearance and workability to stucco, so you can achieve an attractive stucco wall look.

Concrete block walls can also be built with mortar (pages 76 to 79). This is the only option if you're using decorative block (pages 182 to 183) or if you want to leave the blocks exposed.

Everything You Need:

Tools: Aviation snips, mason's trowel, brickset, chisel, maul, mason's string, level, chalk line, line blocks.

Materials: Concrete block, metal ties, wire mesh, type N mortar, surface bonding cement.

How to Lay a Mortarless Block Wall

1 Start with a dry layout of the first course on a concrete footing. Where less than half a block is needed, trim two blocks instead. For example, where 3⅓ block lengths are required, use four blocks, and cut two of them to ⅔ their length. You'll end up with a stronger, more durable wall.

2 Mark the corners of the end blocks on the footing with a pencil. Then, remove the blocks and snap chalk lines to indicate where to lay the mortar bed and the initial course of block.

3 Mist the footing with water, then lay a ⅜"-thick bed of mortar on the footing. Take care to cover only the area inside the reference lines.

4 Lay the first course, starting at one end and placing blocks in the mortar bed with no spacing in between blocks. Use solid-faced block on the ends of the wall, and check the course for level.

Half block

Line block and string

5 Lay subsequent courses one at a time, using a level to check for plumb and line blocks to check for level. Begin courses with solid-face blocks at each end. Use half blocks, to establish a running bond pattern (page 65).

6 If a block requires leveling, cut a piece of corrugated metal tie and slip it underneath. If a block is off by more than ⅛", remove the block, trowel a dab of mortar underneath, and reposition the block.

7 Lay wire mesh over the next to last course. Install the top course, then fill block hollows with mortar and trowel the surface smooth. Complete the project by applying surface bonding cement (pages 214 to 215).

Building a Decorative Block Wall

The decorative-block screen shown here uses the standard techniques for laying brick and block (pages 62 to 79). Half-sized end blocks are used on the exposed end. This wall is topped with masonry caps.

Everything You Need:

Tools: Chalk line, level, line blocks, mason's string, mason's trowel, jointing tool, hammer, open-end wrench.

Materials: Decorative block, type N mortar, end blocks, wall cap, reinforcing strips, ⅜"-dia. J-bolts with oval washers and nuts, metal post anchors, self-tapping masonry anchors, metal pedestals, 4 × 4 posts, 6d galvanized nails, 1" galvanized wire brads, lattice sheets and molding.

1 Make a dry run of the first course of blocks to make sure the layout meets your needs. Use spacers to represent mortar joints. Good planning will minimize the need to cut bricks or blocks, and will speed up your work. Once you have established the layout to your satisfaction, mark layout lines on the concrete base (page 76).

2 With layout lines clearly marked and your brick or block supply nearby, dampen the slab with water, mix the mortar, and throw a mortar bed at one corner or end (pages 30 to 31). Set the first block or brick in the mortar. Tap the block with the handle of your trowel to set it, and check with a level to make sure the block is level and plumb (pages 76 to 77).

3 Complete the first course, maintaining a uniform mortar bed and joint thickness. For the project shown, the first block for the end pillar was also laid. Begin the second course, following your stacking pattern (pages 76 to 79). OPTION: Establish the layout by building corners first, then add blocks or bricks between corners (pages 72 to 75).

4 Smooth out fresh mortar joints (called tooling) within 30 minutes. Use a mortar jointing tool to create clean joints with a consistent look. Tool the horizontal joints first, then tool the vertical joints (page 79). Clean off any excess mortar with a brush after it hardens slightly.

5 Continue laying courses of brick or block, using a mason's string and line blocks to check the alignment (pages 78 to 79).

6 Add reinforcement to the structure as needed (page 68). There are several options for reinforcing brick and block structures—the option you select depends on the type of building materials you are using, and on Building Code regulations. For this project, we embedded metal wire reinforcing strips in the mortar beds for the entire third course.

7 Add a wall cap to increase the strength of the structure, to cover voids in some types of brick or block, and to provide a decorative finish to the project (pages 75 and 79). Let the mortar cure uncovered for at least one week before subjecting it to stress.

How to Add Lattice Panels to a Block Wall

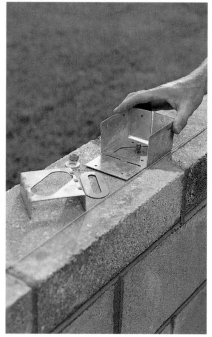

1 While mortar is still wet, install ⅜"-diameter J-bolts into the center of the cap row joints at post locations. About 1" of the bolt should protrude. Pack mortar around the bolt and let it harden. (If mortar already has hardened, see OPTION, step 2.)

2 Align and attach a metal post anchor at each post location. Slip an oval washer over each J-bolt, then attach a nut. OPTION: Attach metal post anchors by driving self-tapping masonry anchors through the predrilled holes in the bottom of the post anchor.

3 Set a metal pedestal into each anchor. The top of the J-bolt should be below the pedestal.

4 Cut a 4 × 4 post for each anchor. Set the post on the pedestal, then bend the open flange up against the post. Make sure the post is plumb, then attach it with 6d galvanized nails.

5 Build lattice panels by cutting 8-ft. sheets of lattice to size and framing them with mitered pieces of lattice molding. Install the panels between posts.

This low patio wall, made with 8 × 8" glass block mortared between concrete block support columns, provides an attractive wind break for an outdoor sitting area while allowing light to pass through.

Building a Glass Block Wall

You may not think of glass as a masonry product, but building a glass block wall is much like laying a mortared brick wall, with two important differences. First, a glass block wall must be supported by another structure and cannot function as a load-bearing wall. Second, glass block cannot be cut, so lay out your project carefully.

You can find glass block, along with a few products that help with the installation, at a specialty distributor or home center. For straight wall sections, use plastic spacers between blocks. The spacers ensure consistent mortar joints and support the weight of the block to prevent mortar from squeezing out before it sets. You'll also find colored glass block (type N) mortar and tints for coloring standard type N mortar. Mix the mortar a little drier than you would for brick; glass won't wick water out of the mortar like brick does.

Because there are many applications for glass block and installation techniques may vary from project to project, ask a glass block retailer or manufacturer for advice about the best products and methods for your project.

Glass block sizes and styles include: bullnose end and corner blocks for finishing exposed edges, and radial blocks for right angles or curves. Glass block textures and patterns offer varying degrees of privacy.

Everything You Need:

Tools: Trowel, level, wire cutters, jointing tool, sponge, pail, nylon-bristle brush, cloth.

Materials: Glass block (8 × 8"), glass block spacers, panel reinforcing wire, anchors, concrete block (6 × 8 × 8"), glass block mortar, type N mortar, 6"-wide capstone, brick sealer.

How to Build a Glass Block Wall

1 Pour an L-shaped footing for the wall (pages 56 to 59). If you'd like to build your wall on an existing foundation, such as a concrete patio, check with your local building department for structural requirements.

2 Dry-lay the first course of block over the center of the footing, using ¼" spacers between blocks to set gaps for the mortar joints. Set the concrete blocks for the support columns, then center the glass block against the concrete blocks. Mark reference lines on the footing and remove the blocks.

T-spacer

3 Lay a bed of mortar inside the reference lines, but do not furrow the mortar (page 30). Set the block for the first course, using T-spacers beneath the blocks. Butter the leading edge of each glass block liberally, using enough mortar to fill the recesses on the sides of both blocks.

4 The spacers will help keep the blocks spaced evenly, but you should check each block with a level to make sure it is level and plumb. Adjust the blocks by tapping lightly with a rubber-tipped trowel handle. Do not adjust blocks with a metal hammer.

5 Fill the gaps between the tops of the blocks with mortar, then set the appropriate spacer in the mortar. Apply a mortar bed and lay the next course.

6 Add reinforcement wire across the entire wall every other course. Lay half (⅛") of the mortar bed, then set the wire in the mortar. Cut the inner rail of reinforcement wire to bend it around corners. Overlap the wire by 6" where more than one piece is needed. Cover the wire with the remaining half of the mortar bed.

7 Use glass block panel anchors every other course to tie the glass block to the support columns. Embed the anchors in the mortar, using the same method as for the reinforcement wire.

8 Tool the mortar joints with a jointing tool when the mortar hardens enough to resist light finger pressure. Remove excess mortar from the glass surfaces before it sets, using a damp sponge. You can also use a nylon- or natural-bristle brush, but take care not to damage the joints.

9 Complete the wall by adding a single course of capstone that is the same width as the concrete support blocks. Option: Use bullnose end blocks for the final course instead of laying a cap.

10 Clean the glass block with a wet sponge to remove grit, rinsing the sponge frequently. Allow the surface to dry, then remove any cloudy residue by rubbing with a clean, dry cloth. After the mortar has cured for two weeks, apply brick sealer to protect it from water damage.

It is easiest to build a dry stone wall with ashlar—stone that has been split into roughly rectangular blocks. Ashlar is stacked in roughly the same running-bond pattern used in brick wall construction (page 65); each stone overlaps a in the previous course. This technique avoids long vertical joints, resulting in a wall that is attractive and also strong.

Building a Dry Stone Wall

Stone walls are beautiful, long-lasting structures that are surprisingly easy to build provided you plan carefully. A low stone wall can be constructed without mortar, using a centuries-old method known as *dry laying*. With this technique, the wall is actually formed by two separate stacks that lean together slightly. The position and weight of the two stacks support each other, forming a single, sturdy wall. A dry stone wall can be built to any length, but must be at least half as wide as it is tall.

You can purchase stone for this project from a quarry or stone supplier, where different sizes, shapes and colors of stone are sold, priced by the ton. The quarry or stone center can also sell you type M mortar—necessary for bonding the capstones to the top of the wall.

Building dry stone walls requires patience and a

fair amount of physical effort. The stones must be sorted by size and shape. You'll probably also need to shape some of the stones to achieve consistent spacing and a general appearance that appeals to you.

To shape a stone, score it, using a circular saw outfitted with a masonry blade (pages 84 to 87). Place a mason's chisel on the score line and strike with a maul until the stone breaks. Wear safety glasses when using stone-cutting tools.

Everything You Need:

Tools: Mason's string, circular saw with masonry blade, mason's chisel, masonry trowel.

Materials: 12" beveled stakes, crushed stone, cut ashlar stone, capstones, type M mortar.

How to Build a Dry Stone Wall

1 Lay out the wall site, using stakes and mason's string. Dig a 6"-deep trench that extends 6" beyond the wall on all sides. Add a 4" crushed stone subbase to the trench, creating a "V" shape by sloping the subbase so the center is about 2" deeper than the edges.

2 Select appropriate stones and lay the first course. Place pairs of stones side by side, flush with the edges of the trench and sloping toward the center. Use stones of similar height; position uneven sides face down. Fill any gaps between the shaping stones with small filler stones.

filler stones

3 Lay the next course, staggering the joints. Use pairs of stones of varying lengths to offset the center joint. Alternate stone length, and keep the height even, stacking pairs of thin stones if necessary to maintain consistent height. Place filler stones in the gaps.

tie stones

4 Every third course, place a tie stone (page 89) every 3 ft. You may need to split the tie stones to length. Check the wall periodically for level.

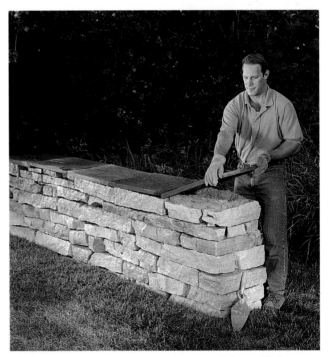

5 Mortar the capstones to the top of the wall, keeping the mortar at least 6" from the edges so it's not visible. Push the capstones together and mortar the cracks in between. Brush off dried excess mortar with a stiff-bristle brush.

Building Entryway Pillars

This 4-ft. pillar was built with 18 courses of brick. A brick cap adds a touch of elegance and protects against rain, ice and snow. You can also build pillars with stone caps, or, as shown on the following pages, use cast concrete caps, which are available in many sizes.

Freestanding pillars are easy to design because you don't have to be concerned about the seasonal shifting of attached walls or other structures. We designed a pair of 12 × 16" pillars using only whole bricks, so you don't need to worry about splitting. These pillars are refined in appearance, but sturdy enough to last for decades.

Once the last course of bricks is in place, you can add a brick or stone cap for a finished look. Or, build two pillars connected by an arch (pages 194 to 197). If you're planning an arch, consider attaching hardware for an iron gate (page 32 to 33). It's far easier to place the hardware in fresh mortar, so make a note of the brick courses where the hardware will go. The settings will look cleaner this way, and the hardware will stay secure for a long time.

Pour footings (pages 56 to 59) that are 4" longer and wider than the pillars on each side. This project calls for 16 × 20" footings.

Everything You Need:

Tools: Level, bricklayer's trowel, jointing tool, aviation snips, wheelbarrow, shovel, hoe, tape measure, pointing chisel.

Materials: Standard modular bricks (4 × 2⅔ × 8"), dowel, type N mortar mix, ¼" wire mesh, capstone or concrete cap, 2 × 2 lumber, ⅜"-thick wood scraps.

Tips for Building Brick Pillars

Use a story pole to maintain consistent mortar joint thickness. Line up a scrap 2 × 2 on a flat tabletop alongside a column of bricks, spaced ⅜" apart. Mark the identical spacing on the 2 × 4. Hold up pole after every few courses to check the mortar joints for consistent thickness.

Cut a straight 2 × 2 to fit tight in the space between the two pillars. As you lay each course for the second pillar, use the 2 × 2 to check the span.

How to Build Brick Pillars

1 Once the footing has cured, dry-lay the first course of five bricks, centered on the footing. Mark reference lines around the bricks.

2 Lay a bed of mortar inside the reference lines and lay the first course (page 72).

(continued next page)

3 Use a pencil or dowel coated with vegetable oil to create a weep hole in the mortar in the first course of bricks. The hole ensures drainage of any moisture that seeps into the pillar. Remember: If you plan to add a gate, review the instructions for installing gate fasteners (page 33) before you proceed beyond the first course of the pillar.

4 Lay the second course, rotating the pattern 180°. Lay additional courses, rotating the pattern 180° with each course. Use the story pole and a level to check each face of the pillar after every other course. (It's important to check frequently, since any errors will be exaggerated with each successive course.)

5 After every fourth course, cut a strip of ¼" wire mesh and place it over a thin bed of mortar. Add another thin bed of mortar on top of the mesh, then add the next course of brick.

6 After every five courses, use a jointing tool to smooth the joints that have hardened enough to resist minimal finger pressure.

7 For the final course, lay the bricks over a bed of mortar and wire mesh. After placing the first two bricks, add an extra brick in the center of the course. Lay the remainder of the bricks to fit snug around it. Fill the remaining joints, and work them with the jointing tool as soon as they become firm.

8 Build the second pillar in the same way as the first. Use the story pole and measuring rod to maintain identical dimensions and spacing.

How to Install a Cap Stone

1 Select a capstone 3" longer and wider than the top of the pillar. Mark reference lines on the bottom for centering the cap. Do not install caps if you are adding an arch to your pillars.

2 Spread a ½"-thick bed of mortar on top of the pillar. Center the cap on the pillar, using the reference lines. Strike the mortar joint under the cap so it's flush with the pillar. NOTE: If mortar squeezes out of the joint, press ⅜"-thick wood scraps into the mortar at each corner to support the cap. Remove the scraps after 24 hours and fill in the gaps with mortar.

If you're building an arch over existing pillars, measure the distance between the pillars at several points. The span must be the same at each point in order for the pillars to serve as strong supports for your arch.

Adding an Arch to Entryway Pillars

Building an arch over a pair of pillars is a challenging task made easier with a simple, semi-circular plywood form. With the form in place, you can create a symmetrical arch by laying bricks along the form's curved edge. Select bricks equal in length to those used in the pillars.

When building new pillars (pages 190 to 193), use the colors and textures of your home exterior and landscape to guide your choice of brick. Brickyards sells mortar tint (page 31) to complement the color of your bricks. Once you settle on the amount of tint to add to the mortar, record the

recipe, so you can maintain a consistent color in every batch.

Everything You Need:

Tools: Joint chisel, mason's hammer, pry bar, jig saw, circular saw, drill, compass, level, mason's string, trowel, jointing tool, tuck-pointer.

Materials: ¾" plywood, ¼" plywood, wallboard screws (1" and 2"), bricks, type N mortar mix, 2 x 4 and 2 x 8 lumber, shims.

How to Build a Form for an Arch

1 Determine the distance between the inside edges of the tops of your pillars. Divide the distance in half, then subtract ¼". Use this as the radius in step 2.

2 Mark a point at the center of a sheet of ¾" plywood. Use a pencil and a piece of string to scribe the circle on the plywood, using the radius calculated in step 1. Cut out the circle with a jigsaw. Then mark a line through the center point of the circle and cut the circle in half with a jig saw or a circular saw.

3 Construct the form by bracing the two semicircles, using 2" wallboard screws and 2 × 4s. To calculate the length of the 2 × 4 braces, subtract the combined thickness of the plywood sheets — 1½"—from the width of the pillars, and cut the braces to length. Cover the top of the form with ¼" plywood, attached with 1" wallboard screws.

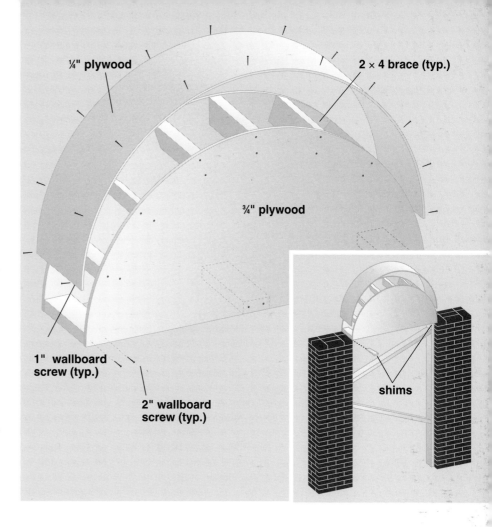

¼" plywood

2 × 4 brace (typ.)

¾" plywood

1" wallboard screw (typ.)

2" wallboard screw (typ.)

shims

How to Build a Brick Arch

Tip: If your pillars are capped, remove the caps before building an arch. Chip out the old mortar from underneath, using a hammer and joint chisel. With a helper nearby to support the cap, use a pry bar and shims to remove each cap from the pillar.

1 To determine brick spacing, start by centering a brick at the peak and placing a compass point at one edge. With the compass set to the width of one brick plus ¼", mark the form with the pencil.

2 Place the compass point on this new mark and make another mark along the curve. Continue making marks along the curve until less than a brick's width remains.

(continued next page)

3 Divide this remaining width by the number of compass marks, and increase the compass setting by this amount. Using a different color, make final reference marks to either side of the peak. Extend the pencil lines across the curved surface of the form and onto the far edge.

4 Cut two 2 × 8 braces, ½" shorter than pillar height, and prop one against each pillar with 2 × 4 cross braces. Place shims on top of each 2 × 8 to raise the form so its bottom is even with the tops of the pillars. Rest the plywood form on the braces.

5 Mix mortar and trowel a narrow ⅜" layer on top of one pillar. Place one brick, then rap the top with a trowel handle to settle it. Butter the bottom of each subsequent brick, and place it in position.

6 Place five bricks, then tack a string to the center point of the form on each side, and use the strings to check each brick's alignment. Take care not to dislodge other bricks as you tap a brick into position.

7 To balance the weight on the form, switch to the other side. Continue alternating until space for one brick remains. Smooth previous joints with a jointing tool as they become firm.

8 Butter the center, or *keystone*, brick as accurately as possible and ease it into place. Smooth the remaining joints with a jointing tool.

9 Lay a bed of mortar over the first course, then lay the second course halfway up each side, maintaining the same mortar joint thickness as in the first layer. Some of the joints will be staggered, adding strength to the arch.

10 Dry-lay several more bricks on one side—using shims as substitutes for mortar joints—to check the amount of space remaining. Remove the shims and lay the final bricks with mortar, then smooth the joints with a jointing tool.

11 Leave the form in place for a week, misting occasionally. Carefully remove the braces and form. Tuck-point and smooth the joints on the underside of the arch (page 31).

A moon window is just about the most dramatic garden element you can build. We constructed the wall shown here using cut ashlar mortared around a semicircular form, but using brick is also an option. Once the bottom half of the window has set up, the form is flipped and the top stones are placed. The construction technique for the form is the same one used in building an arch (pages 195 to 197).

Building a Stone Moon Window

You can build circular openings into brick or stone walls, using a single semicircular wood form. Moon windows can be built to any dimension, although lifting and placing stones is more difficult as the project grows larger, while tapering stones to fit is a greater challenge as the circle gets smaller. To minimize the need for cutting and lifting stone, we built this window 2 ft. in diameter atop an existing stone wall. Before doing this, you'll need to check with your local building inspector regarding restrictions on wall height, footings (pages 56 to 57), and other design considerations. You may need to modify the dimensions to conform with the local Building Code.

Make sure to have at least one helper on hand. Building with stone is always physically demanding, and steps such as installing the brace and form (opposite page) require a helper.

Everything You Need:

Tools: Jig saw, circular saw, drill, tape measure, level, mortar box, mason's hoe, trowels, jointing tool or tuck-pointer, mortar bag, stone chisel, maul.

Materials: ¾" plywood, ¼" plywood, wallboard screws (1" and 2"), tapered shims, 2 × 4 and 2 × 8 lumber, 4 × 4 posts, type M mortar (stiff mix), ashlar stone.

How to Build a Stone Moon Window

1 Build a plywood form, following the instructions on page 195. Select stones for the top of the circle with sides that are squared off or slightly tapered. Dry-lay the stones around the outside of the form, spacing the stones with shims that are roughly ¼" thick at their narrow end.

2 Number each stone and a corresponding point on the form, using chalk, then set the stones aside. Turn the form around, and label a second set of stones for the bottom of the circle. Tip: to avoid confusion, use letters to label the bottom set of stones instead of numbers.

3 Prepare a stiff mix of type M mortar (pages 29 and 31) and lay a ½"-thick mortar bed on top of the wall for the base of the circle. Center the stone that will be at the base of the circle in the mortar.

4 Set the form on top of the stone, and brace the form by constructing a sturdy 2 × 4 scaffold and secure it by constructing a bracing structure made from 4 × 4 posts and 2 × 4 lumber. We used pairs of 2 × 4s nailed together for lengthwise supports. Check the form for level in both directions, and adjust the braces as required. Screw the braces to the form, so the edges are at least ¼" in from the edges of the form.

(continued next page)

5 Extend the mortar bed along the wall and add stones, buttering one end of each stone, and tapping them into place with a trowel. Keep the joint width consistent with the existing wall, but set the depth of new joints at about 1", to allow for tuck-pointing.

6 Attach mason's string at the center of the front and back of the form and use the strings to check the alignment of each stone.

7 Stagger the joints as you build upward and outward. Alternate large and small stones for maximum strength and a natural look. Stop occasionally to smooth joints that have hardened enough to resist minimal finger pressure.

8 If large bumps or curves interfere as you lay stones around the circle, dress those stones (page 85 to 87), as necessary, so the sides are roughly squared off.

9 Once you've laid stones about ½" beyond the top edge of the form, disassemble the bracing.

10 Invert the form on top of the wall in preparation for laying the top half of the circle. The bottom edge of the form should be set roughly ½" higher than the top of the lower half of the circle. Check the braces for level (both lengthwise and widthwise), and adjust them as necessary and reattach them to the posts.

11 Lay stones around the circle, working from the bottom up, so the top, or keystone, is laid last. If mortar oozes from the joints, insert temporary shims. Remove the shims after 2 hours, and pack the voids with mortar.

12 Once the keystone is in place, smooth the remaining joints. Let the wall set up overnight, then mist it several times a day for a week. Remove the form.

13 Remove any excess mortar from the joints inside the circle. Mist lightly, then tuck-point all joints with stiff mortar so they are of equal depth (page 31).

14 Once the joints reach a putty-like consistency, tool them with a jointing tool. Let the mortar harden overnight. Mist the wall for five more days.

Terraced retaining walls work well on steep hillsides. Two or more short retaining walls are easier to install and more stable than a single, tall retaining wall. Construct the terraces so each wall is no higher than 3 ft.

Building Retaining Walls

Retaining walls are often used to level a yard or to prevent erosion on a hillside. In a flat yard, you can build a low retaining wall and fill in behind it to create a raised planting bed.

Retaining walls taller than 3 ft. are subject to thousands of pounds of pressure from the weight of the soil and water, so they require special building techniques that are best left to a professional. If you have a tall hillside, it's best to terrace the hill with several short walls.

The retaining walls in this section were built with either interlocking block or cut stone. These durable materials are easy to work with. No matter what material you use, your wall can be damaged if water saturates the soil behind it, so make sure you include the proper drainage features (page 203). You may need to dig a drainage swale (page 18 to 19) before building in low-lying areas.

Interlocking block is available in several styles at home and garden centers. Many types have a natural rock finish, combining the texture of cut stone with the uniformity of concrete block.

Natural stone walls usually are laid without mor-tar, although the last one or two courses are usually mortared for greater strength. With its flat surfaces, cut stone is much easier to build with than rubble or field stone. Make sure you have plenty of broad, flat stones to use as tie-stones, capstones (pages 88 to 89), and *deadman* stones (page 207). Dry stone walls require no concrete footings. Several inches of compactible gravel are used instead.

NOTE: Before excavating, check with local utility companies to make sure there are no underground pipes or cables running through the site.

Everything You Need:

Tools: Shovel, wheelbarrow, rake, line level, mason's string, hand tamper, rented tamping machine, maul, masonry chisel, circular saw and masonry blade, level, caulk gun (block wall), trowel (stone wall).

Materials: Stakes, landscape fabric, compactible gravel, perforated drain pipe, crushed stone, construction adhesive (block wall), type M mortar (stone wall).

Options for Positioning a Retaining Wall

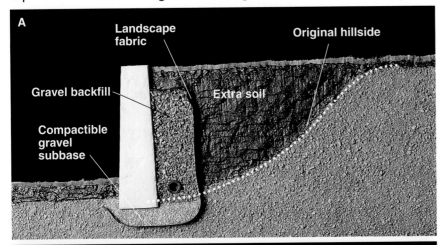

A — Landscape fabric, Gravel backfill, Compactible gravel subbase, Extra soil, Original hillside

B — Soil removed from base of hill, Original hillside, Compactible gravel subbase

(A) Increase the level area above the wall by positioning the wall well forward from the top of the hill. Fill in behind the wall with extra soil, which is available from sand-and-gravel companies.

(B) Keep the basic shape of your yard by positioning the wall near the top of the hillside. Use the soil removed at the base of the hill to fill in near the top of the wall.

Structural features for all retaining walls include: a compactible gravel subbase to make a solid footing for the wall, crushed stone backfill and a perforated drain pipe to improve drainage behind the wall, and landscape fabric to keep the loose soil from washing into and clogging the gravel backfill.

Tips for Building Retaining Walls

Backfill with crushed stone and install a perforated drain pipe about 6" above the bottom of the backfill. Vent the pipe to the side or bottom of the retaining wall, where runoff water can flow away from the hillside without causing erosion.

Make a stepped trench when the ends of a retaining wall must blend into an existing hillside. Retaining walls often are designed so the ends curve or turn back into the slope.

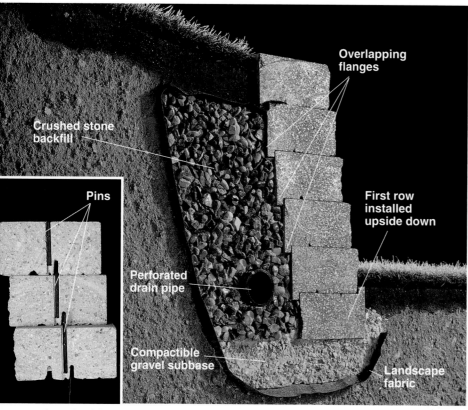

Crushed stone backfill

Overlapping flanges

Pins

First row installed upside down

Perforated drain pipe

Compactible gravel subbase

Landscape fabric

Interlocking wall blocks do not need mortar. Some types are held together with a system of overlapping flanges that automatically set the backward angle (batter) as the blocks are stacked. Other types of blocks use a pinning system (inset).

1 Excavate the hillside, if necessary (page 203). Allow 12" of space for crushed stone backfill between the back of the wall and the hillside. Use stakes to mark the front edge of the wall. Connect the stakes with mason's string, and use a line level to check for level.

2 Dig out the bottom of the excavation below ground level, so it is 6" lower than the height of the block. For example, if you use 6"-thick block, dig down 12". Measure down from the string to make sure the bottom base is level.

3 Line the excavation with strips of landscape fabric cut 3 ft. longer than the planned height of the wall. Make sure all seams overlap by at least 6".

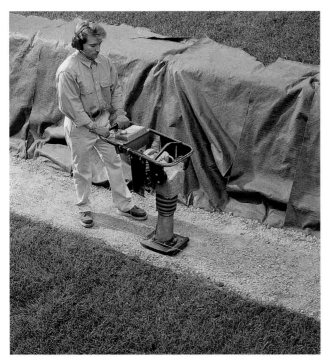

4 Spread a 6" layer of compactible gravel over the bottom of the excavation as a subbase and pack it thoroughly. A rented tamping machine, or *jumping jack*, works better than a hand tamper for packing the subbase.

5 Lay the first course of block, aligning the front edges with the mason's string. (When using flanged block, place the first course upside down and backward.) Check frequently with a level, and adjust, if necessary, by adding or removing subbase material below the blocks.

6 Lay the second course of block according to manufacturer's instructions, checking to make sure the blocks are level. (Lay flanged block with the flanges tight against the underlying course.) Add 3 to 4" of gravel behind the block, and pack it with a hand tamper.

7 Make half-blocks for the corners and ends of a wall, and use them to stagger vertical joints between courses. Score full blocks with a circular saw and masonry blade, then break the blocks along the scored line with a maul and chisel (page 71).

(continued next page)

8 Add and tamp crushed stone, as needed, to create a slight downward pitch (about ¼" of height per foot of pipe) leading to the drain pipe outlet. Place the drain pipe on the crushed stone, 6" behind the wall, with the perforations face down. Make sure the pipe outlet is unobstructed (page 203). Lay courses of block until the wall is about 18" above ground level, staggering the vertical joints.

9 Fill behind the wall with crushed stone, and pack it thoroughly with the hand tamper. Lay the remaining courses of block, except for the cap row, backfilling with crushed stone and packing with the tamper as you go.

10 Before laying the cap block, fold the end of the landscape fabric over the crushed stone backfill. Add a thin layer of topsoil over the fabric, then pack it thoroughly with a hand tamper. Fold any excess landscape fabric back over the tamped soil.

11 Apply construction adhesive to the top course of block, then lay the cap block. Use topsoil to fill in behind the wall and to fill in the base at the front of the wall. Install sod or plants, as desired.

How to Build a Retaining Wall Using Natural Stone

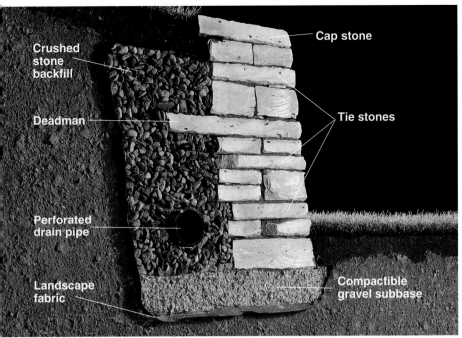

Crushed stone backfill

Deadman

Perforated drain pipe

Landscape fabric

Cap stone

Tie stones

Compactible gravel subbase

Cut stone has flat, smooth surfaces for easy stacking. For a stable retaining wall, alternate courses of tie stones that span the entire width of the wall with rows of smaller stones. Install extra-long stones (called *deadmen*) that extend back into the crushed stone backfill, spaced every 4 ft. to 6 ft. Prepare the site (steps 1 to 4, pages 204 to 205). The top of the compacted subbase should be about 6" below ground level.

1 Sort the stones by size and shape. It's the only way to survey your supply and make sure you have enough long tie stones to build a strong wall. Trim irregular stones to fit (pages 86 to 87)

2 Lay courses of stone, following the same techniques for backfilling and drainage as for interlocking blocks (steps 6 to 10, pages 205 to 206). Batter the wall by setting each course about ½" back from the preceding course (pages 89 and 204). For stability, work tie-stones and deadmen into the wall, and stagger the vertical joints between courses. Use the heaviest stones for the base of the wall.

3 Before laying the capstone, mix type M mortar (pages 29 to 31) and apply a thick bed along the top of the final course, keeping the mortar a few inches from the front face of the wall. This technique is called *blind mortaring*. Press the capstones into the mortar. Allow the mortar to cure for at least a day, then finish backfilling the wall (step 11, opposite page).

Update the exterior of your house with brick, stone or stucco veneer. Whether installed to cover an unattractive foundation or to accent an otherwise ordinary exterior, veneers add color and texture to your house. They also add weight to a wall, so ask an inspector about Building Code rules before you start.

Finishing House & Garden Walls

Masonry materials are ideal for protecting and enhancing the look of exterior walls, both new and old. If house siding has deteriorated, you can tear it off and install a lightweight brick veneer, using mortar and wall ties (pages 210 to 213). If you build an addition, you can use stucco to match or complement the materials on existing walls (pages 220 to 221). Stucco is also easy to repair or restore. Thin veneers of natural or manufactured stone are growing rapidly in popularity because they are easy to work with and add a touch of grandeur to any structure. These materials all work well on garden walls, too. With brick, stone, or stucco, you can turn an ordinary concrete block wall into an attractive element of your garden. With concrete block and super-strong surface bonding cement (pages 214 to 215), you can build a wall with a stucco-style surface, using no mortar at all.

Tips for Planning:

• Use brick or stone veneer as a decorative accent on the front face or entry area of your house. Installing veneer around an entire house is a demanding project best left to a professional.

• Ask your local building inspector about allowable height, reinforcement, use of wall ties, space between veneer and wall sheathing, drainage, and specifications for metal support shelves (page 210). A building permit may be required.

• Cut bricks before you start. With stone, do a dry run on a flat surface before you start.

• Examine the area around your foundation. Builders often install a concrete ledge just below grade as a base for veneer. If your house has no base, attach a metal support shelf to the foundation (page 210).

Options for Finishing Exterior Walls

Renew an old foundation by applying brick or stone veneer from ground level up to the sill plate. The foundation must be free from structural damage.

Photo courtesy of CULTURED STONE CORPORATION

Veneer stone may consist of thin cuts of quarried stone or tinted concrete blocks that look like natural stone but are lighter and easier to install.

Full-wall veneer is applied from the foundation to the roof soffit. Because of the extreme weight of full-wall veneer, extensive reinforcement is required. Installation is not generally recommended for do-it-yourselfers; consult a professional.

Stucco is a durable finish that can be tinted to blend with surroundings. Window trim is removed to apply stucco to house walls. Narrow trowel cuts under the trim serve as control joints, preventing large cracks from appearing later.

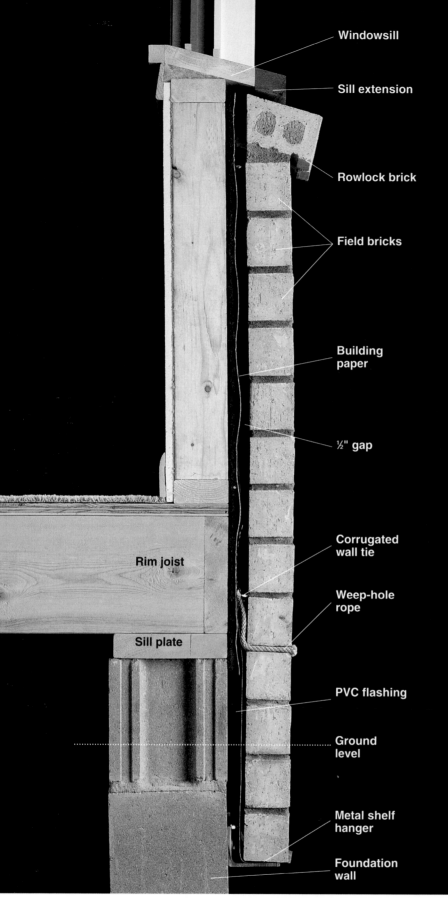

Windowsill

Sill extension

Rowlock brick

Field bricks

Building paper

½" gap

Rim joist

Corrugated wall tie

Weep-hole rope

Sill plate

PVC flashing

Ground level

Metal shelf hanger

Foundation wall

Anatomy of a brick veneer facade: Queen-sized bricks are stacked onto a metal or concrete shelf and connected to the foundation and walls with metal ties. *Rowlock* bricks are cut to follow the slope of the windowsills, then laid on edge over the top course of bricks.

Finishing Walls with Brick

Brick veneer is essentially a brick wall built around the exterior walls of a house. It is attached to the house with metal wall ties and supported by a metal shelf hanger on the foundation. It is best to use queen-size bricks for veneer projects because they are thinner than standard construction bricks. This means less weight for the house walls to support. Even so, brick veneer is quite heavy. Ask your local building inspector about Building Code rules that apply to your project. In the project shown here, brick veneer is installed over the foundation walls and side walls, up to the bottoms of the windowsills on the first floor of the house. The siding materials in these areas are removed before installing the brick.

You need to construct a story pole before you start laying brick so you can check your work as you go along to be sure your mortar joints are of a consistent thickness. A standard ⅜" gap is used in the project shown here.

Everything You Need:

Tools: Hammer, circular saw, chisel, maul, level, drill, socket wrench set, staple gun, mason's trowel, masonry hoe, mortar box, mason's chisel, maul.

Materials: pressure-treated 2 × 4s, ⅜ × 4" lag screws and washers, 2 × 2, lead sleeve anchors, angle iron for metal shelf supports, 30 mil PVC roll flashing, corrugated metal wall ties, brickmold for sill extensions, sill-nosing trim, type N mortar, bricks, ⅜-dia. cotton rope.

How to Install Brick Veneer

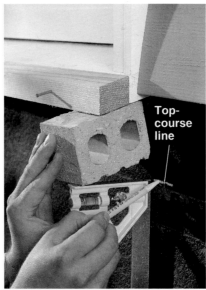

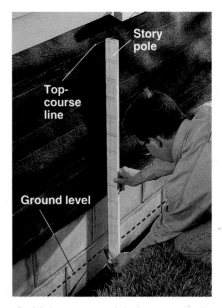

1 Remove all siding materials in the area you plan to finish with brick veneer. Install a wooden extension onto the windowsill. Before you start laying out the project, cut the wood for the sill extension from a pressure-treated 2 × 4. Tack the extension onto the sill temporarily.

2 Precut the bricks to follow the slope of the sill and overhang the field brick by 2". Position this rowlock brick directly under the sill extension. Use a level to transfer the lowest point on the brick onto the sheathing (marking the height for the top course of veneer brick in the field area). Use a level to extend the line. Remove the sill extensions.

3 Make a story pole long enough to span your project area. Mark the pole with ⅜" joints between bricks (pages 39 and 191). Dig a 12"-wide, 12"-deep trench. Position the pole so the top-course line on the sheathing aligns with a top mark for a brick on the pole. Mark a line for the first course on the wall, below ground level.

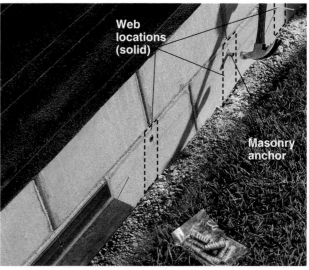

4 Extend the mark for the first-course height across the foundation wall, using a level as a guide. Measure the thickness of the metal shelf (usually ¼"), and drill pilot holes for 10d nails into the foundation at 16" intervals along the first-course line, far enough below the line to allow for the thickness of the shelf. Slip nails into the pilot holes to create temporary support for the shelf.

5 Set the metal shelf onto the temporary supports; mark the location of the center web of each block onto the vertical face of the shelf. Remove the shelf and drill ⅜"-diameter holes for lag screws at the web marks. Set the shelf back onto the temporary supports and outline the predrilled holes onto the blocks. Remove the shelf and drill holes for the masonry anchors into the foundation, using a masonry bit. Drive the masonry anchors into the holes.

(continued next page)

6 Reposition the shelf on the supports so the predrilled holes align with the masonry anchors. Attach the shelf to the foundation wall with ⅜ × 4" lag screws and washers. Allow 1⁄16" for an expansion joint between shelf sections. Remove the temporary support nails.

7 After all sections of the metal shelf are attached, staple 30 mil PVC flashing above the foundation wall so it laps over the metal shelf.

8 Test-fit the first course on the shelf. Work in from the ends, using spacers to set the gaps between bricks. You may need to cut the final brick for the course. Or, choose a pattern such as running bond (page 65) that uses cut bricks.

9 Build up the corners two courses above ground level, then attach line blocks and mason's string to the end bricks (pages 74 to 75) and fill in the field bricks so they align with the strings. Every 30 minutes, smooth mortar joints that are firm.

10 Attach another course of PVC flashing to the wall so it covers the top course of bricks, then staple building paper to the wall so it overlaps the top edge of the PVC flashing by at least 12". Mark wall-stud locations on the building paper.

11 Use the story pole to mark layout lines for the tops of every fifth course of bricks. Attach corrugated metal wall ties to the sheathing where the brick lines meet the marked wall-stud locations.

12 Fill in the next course of bricks, applying mortar directly onto the PVC flashing. At every third mortar joint in this course, tack a 10" piece of ⅜"-dia. cotton rope to the sheathing so it extends all the way through the bottom of the joint, creating a weep hole for drainage. Embed the metal wall ties in the mortar beds applied to this course.

13 Add courses of bricks, building up corners first, then filling in the field. Imbed the wall ties into the mortar beds as you reach them. Use corner blocks and a mason's string to verify the alignment, and check frequently with a 4-ft. level to make sure the veneer is plumb.

14 Apply a ½"-thick mortar bed to the top course, and begin laying the "rowlock" bricks with the cut ends against the wall. Apply a layer of mortar to the bottom of each rowlock brick, then press the brick up against the sheathing, with the top edge following the slope of the windowsills.

Sill-nosing trim

15 Finish-nail the sill extensions (step 1, page 211) to the windowsills, and nail sill-nosing trim to the siding to cover any gaps above the rowlock course. Fill cores of exposed rowlock blocks with mortar, and caulk any gaps around the veneer with silicone caulk.

Mix small batches of dry surface bonding cement, water and concrete acrylic fortifier, according to the manufacturer's instructions, until you get a feel for how much coating you can apply before it hardens. An accelerant in the cement causes the mix to harden quickly—within 30 to 90 minutes, depending on weather conditions. To complement surrounding yard features, you can tint the cement before applying it (page 31).

Finishing Walls with Cement

Surface bonding cement is a stucco-like compound that you can use to build new walls or to renew old ones. What distinguishes surface bonding cement from stucco is the addition of fiberglass to the blend of portland cement and sand. The dry mixture is combined with water and acrylic fortifier to form a cement plaster that can bond with either brick or block for an attractive, water-resistant coating that is strong enough for building block walls without mortar joints (pages 180 to 181).

Whether you're building a new wall or applying a decorative coating to an old one, make sure you have a very clean surface, with no crumbling masonry, so the coating can form a durable bond. Because surface bonding cement dries quickly, it's important to mist the brick or block with water before applying the cement so the cement dries slowly. As with most masonry pro-

jects, the need to dampen the wall increases in very dry weather.

The project presented here is designed for building low freestanding walls—*up to four feet in height.* If you're planning to use surface bonding cement to support higher walls or load-bearing walls, such as foundation or retaining walls, talk to your building inspector about local code requirements.

Everything You Need:

Tools: Garden hose with spray attachment, bucket, wheelbarrow, mortar hawk, square-end trowel, groover.

Materials: Surface bonding cement, concrete acrylic fortifier, tint (optional).

How to Finish Walls with Surface-bonding Cement

1 Starting near the top of the wall, mist a 2 × 5 ft. section on one side of the wall with water to prevent the blocks from absorbing moisture from the cement once the coating is applied.

2 Mix the cement in small batches, according to the manufacturer's instructions, and apply a ⅟₁₆"- to ⅛"-thick layer to the damp blocks, using a square-end trowel. Spread the cement evenly by angling the trowel slightly and making broad upward strokes.

3 Use a wet trowel to smooth the surface, and to create the texture of your choice. Rinse the trowel frequently to keep it clean and wet.

4 To prevent random cracking, use a groover (page 49) to cut control joints from top to bottom, every 4 ft. for a 2-ft.-high wall, every 8 ft. for a 4-ft.-high wall. Seal the hardened joints with silicone caulk.

Find the square footage of veneer stone required for your project by multiplying the length by the height of the area. Subtract the square footage of window and door openings and corner pieces. One linear foot of corner pieces covers approximately ¾ of a square foot of flat area, so you can reduce the square footage of flat stone required by ¾ sq. ft. for each linear foot of inside or outside corner. It's best to increase your estimate by 5 to 10 percent to allow for trimming.

Finishing Walls with Veneer Stone

If you want the look of stone on your house without the rigors of cutting and moving heavy materials, veneer stone is ideal. Two types of veneer are available. One is natural stone that has been cut into thin pieces designed for finishing walls, hearths, and other surfaces. The other is made from concrete that is molded and tinted to look like natural stone, but is even lighter and easier to apply to these surfaces.

Whether you use natural or manufactured veneer, wet each stone, then apply mortar to the back before pressing it onto the mortared wall. Wetting and mortaring a stone (called *parging*) results in maximum adhesion between the stone and the wall. The challenge is to arrange the stones so that large and small stones and various hues and shapes alternate across the span of the wall.

This project is designed for installing veneer stone over plywood sheathing, which has the strength to support layers of building paper, lath, and veneer. If your walls are covered with

fiberboard or any other type of sheathing, ask the veneer manufacturer for recommendations.

NOTE: Installing from the top down makes cleanup easier, since it reduces the amount of splatter on preceding courses. However, manufacturers advise bottom-up installation for some veneers. Read the manufacturer's guidelines carefully before you begin.

Everything You Need:

Tools: Hammer or staple gun, drill, wheelbarrow, mortar, hoe, square-end trowel, circular saw, wide-mouth nippers or mason's hammer, dust mask, level, jointing tool, mortar bag, spray bottle, whisk broom.

Materials: Type M mortar mix, mortar tint (optional), 15-lb. building paper, expanded galvanized metal lath (diamond mesh, minimum 2.5-lb.), 1½" (minimum) galvanized roofing nails or heavy-duty staples, 2 × 4 lumber.

How to Finish Walls with Stone Veneer

1 Cover the wall with sheets of building paper, overlapped by 4". Nail or staple lath every 6" into the wall studs and midway between studs. Nails or staples should penetrate 1" into the studs. Paper and lath must extend at least 16" around corners where veneer is installed.

2 Stake a level 2 × 4 against the foundation as a temporary shelf to keep the bottom edge of the veneer 4" above grade. The gap between the bottom course and the ground will reduce staining of the veneer by plants and soil.

3 Spread out materials on the ground so you can select pieces of varying size, shape, and color, and create contrast in the overall appearance. Alternate the use of large and small, heavily textured and smooth, and thick and thin pieces.

4 Mix a batch of type M mortar that is firm, but still moist (pages 29 and 31). Mortar that is too dry or too wet is hard to work with and may fail to bond properly.

(continued on next page)

5 Use a square-end trowel to press a ½" to ¾" layer of mortar into the lath. To ensure that mortar doesn't set up too quickly, start with a 5 sq. ft. area. Once you determine your pace, you can mortar larger areas. NOTE: You can mix in small amounts of water to retemper mortar that has begun to thicken.

6 Install corner pieces first, alternating long and short *legs*. Wet and parge (page 216) each piece, then press it firmly against the freshly mortared wall so some mortar squeezes out. Joints between stones should be no wider than ½" and should remain as consistent as possible across the wall.

7 Once the corner pieces are in place, install flat pieces, working toward the center of the wall.

8 If mortar becomes smeared on a stone, remove it with a whisk broom or soft-bristle brush after the mortar has begun to dry. Never use a wire brush or a wet brush of any kind.

9 Trim natural stone using standard stone-cutting techniques (pages 84 to 87). To cut manufactured stone, use wide-mouth nippers or a mason's hammer to trim and shape pieces to fit. Do your best to limit trimming so that each piece retains its natural look.

10 You can hide cut edges that are well above or below eye level simply by rotating a stone. If an edge remains visible, use mortar to cover. Let the mortar cure for 24 hours, then remove the 2 × 4 and stakes, taking care not to dislodge any stones.

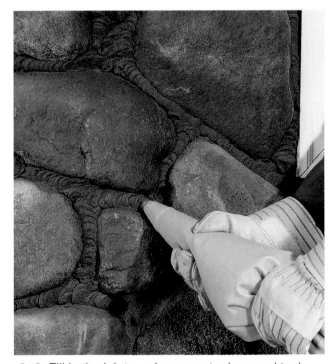

11 Fill in the joints, using a mortar bag and tuck-pointing mortar (page 31), once the wall is covered in veneer, but take extra care to avoid smearing the mortar. You can tint the tuck-pointing mortar to complement the veneer.

12 Smooth the joints with a jointing tool once the mortar is firm. Once the mortar is dry to the touch, use a dry whisk broom to remove loose mortar—water or chemicals can leave a permanent stain.

Finishing Walls with Stucco

Refinishing an entire house with stucco is a demanding job not well suited to even the most committed homeowner. It's a job best left to a stucco mason, who can complete most stucco projects in less than a week. But finishing the walls of a small addition, garage, or shed can be quite satisfying. You can use stucco to match existing walls or to create a texture that complements stone, cedar shakes, or other types of siding.

Good wall preparation is the first step for an attractive, durable finish. If the walls are wood, attach building paper and metal lath to create a tight seal and a gripping surface for the stucco. Concrete block walls are already fairly watertight and are rough enough that stucco can be applied directly to the block. During new block construction, make the mortar joints flush with the blocks in preparation for a stucco finish.

Once you've prepared the wall surface, plan to spend several days applying the three stucco coats—scratch coat, brown coat, and finish coat—that guarantee a tight seal and a professional appearance.

If the original walls of your house are finished with stucco, you'll probably need to tint your finish coat to match. Even if the stucco originally applied to your house was white, that finish has probably darkened considerably. Tinting is the best way to match the new with the old. Follow the manufacturer's instructions for the tint you purchase, and plan to experiment until you find a good match. Let each test batch dry thoroughly before you settle on the proportions. Keep notes as you test so you can reproduce the results for each subsequent batch of stucco.

By adding tint to the mixture, you can produce just about any color stucco you desire, from a subtle off-white to a stately blue.

Everything You Need:

Tools: Cement mixer, wheelbarrow, mortar hawk, mason's trowel, square-end trowel, darby or long wood float, hammer, staple gun, level, utility knife, aviation snips, spade, bucket, fine-tined metal rake.

Materials: Building paper, expanded galvanized metal lath (diamond mesh, minimum 2.5 lb.), 1½" galvanized nails, 1½" wire nails, staples, stucco mix, 1½" wire nails, 1 × 2.

How to Finish a Wall with Stucco

1 Prepare the wall by attaching building paper, metal lath, and edging (pages 92 to 94). Staple the building paper to the entire wall, and trim the excess with a utility knife. Trim the lath and edging to size, using aviation snips, and nail them to the wall. Rub your hand down the lath; it will feel rough when it is positioned upright. Check the edging for level.

2 Mix the scratch coat (page 92), adding water and kneading it with a trowel until it forms a workable paste (pages 94 to 95). Beginning at either the top or the bottom of the wall, hold the mortar hawk close the wall and press mud into the mesh with a square-end trowel. Press firmly to fill any voids, and cover the mesh completely.

3 Wait for the scratch coat to harden enough so that an impression remains when you press on the stucco. Rough up the surface by making shallow horizontal scratches the length of the wall. You can make a scratching tool by pounding a row of 1½" wire nails through a 1 × 2.

4 Mist the surface occasionally for 48 hours. Mix and apply the brown coat approximately ⅜" thick, then level the entire surface with a wood darby to provide a roughened gripping surface for the finish coat.

5 Mix the finish coat, adding tint as required, and slightly more water than in previous coats. The mix should still sit on the mortar hawk without running. Apply finish coat so the edging is fully embedded (approximately ⅛" thick).

6 Finish the surface by throwing stucco at the wall with a whisk broom, then flattening the stucco with a trowel (page 95). Wait 24 hours for the finish coat to set up, then mist 2 to 3 times a day for two days, and once a day for another three days.

Building Landscape Accents

Masonry materials are ideal for creating and installing outdoor accents—from planters to barbecues—that are functional and attractive. Masonry lasts a long time, is easy to maintain, and, as this book has demonstrated, can be fashioned in a myriad of ways to blend with its surroundings. Because of the range of masonry materials, you can build small accent pieces and larger structures to complement just about any landscape.

Half the challenge—and half the enjoyment—of creating masonry accents is in the design stage. Since each piece is presumably intended for a specific location, spend some time thinking about the other elements in that area. The list includes everything from grass, gardens, and paths to driveways, garages and the permanent structure of your house. Step back from the designated area and view it from several angles to get a clear sense of how your accent piece will fit in.

Bear in mind some practical considerations that will affect your landscape accent as well. Shade, prevailing winds, and ground moisture (pages 18 to 19) can all play a role in how much use an accent piece gets. A birdbath may be ideal for a wet low-lying area that is easily seen but seldom used for other purposes. A barbecue, on the other hand, belongs in a dry, comfortable spot, where you can entertain guests and have easy access to the kitchen.

Tips on Installing Landscape Accents

A birdbath (pages 224 to 226) can blend with almost any surroundings. The key is to place it where you can enjoy the sight of the birds, but still offer enough shade to attract them.

Flower planters can be moveable units that stand alone (pages 227 to 229) or permanent structures that attached to walls, patios, or landings (pages 230 to 231). Isolation boards separate this planter from the adjacent wall and landing to allow each structure to shift independently during freezing and thawing.

A driveway marker (page 232 to 233), should be proportional to the driveway and use materials that complement its surroundings. The design of a masonry project should always take into account the scale of nearby landscape elements.

A brick barbeque (pages 234 to 237) should be positioned near the kitchen and where there is space for guest to gather. Take into account the prevailing winds to avoid a smoke-out of your guests or your house.

Building a
Hypertufa Birdbath

This birdbath is sturdy, inexpensive, and easy to build. It is designed with modular sections that are easy to carry and store, so you can move it into the garage or basement for the winter. Once assembled, the sections are held in place by PVC fittings, so it can withstand high winds or jostling by children or animals.

Once cured, hypertufa has an attractive patina. You can enhance the aged look by chipping off the corners with a maul and chisel (step 5, page 226), or by encouraging moss to grow on it (page 229). When building a birdbath, it is especially important to use a water-resistant hypertufa recipe (pages 96 to 97). Seal the basin with 2 to 3 coats of concrete sealer. A thin layer of portland cement is also effective, but less attractive.

This attractive birdbath is built in three detachable sections, making it simple to disassemble and store for the winter. Each of the three sections is poured separately, so construction is quite simple.

Everything You Need:

Tools: Jig saw, power screwdriver, hacksaw, hoe, trowel, straightedge.

Materials: 2" polystyrene insulation board, gaffer's tape, 3½" wallboard screws, vegetable oil or commercial release agent, 2" PVC pipe, 2" PVC pipe cap, portland cement, peat moss, mason's sand, shallow plastic bowl, plastic sheeting.

How to Build a Hypertufa Birdbath

1 Follow the diagram (right) to mark dimensions for the forms onto polystyrene insulation. Cut out the pieces and construct the forms, reinforcing the joints with wallboard screws. The goal is to create a 15 × 15 × 3½" base, a 7¾ × 7¾ × 22" pedestal, and a 15 × 15 × 3½" basin to rest on top of the pedestal. Support the joints by wrapping them with gaffer's tape. NOTE: The wet hypertufa puts quite a bit of pressure on the walls of the form. You can fashion a collar around the form with 1 × 2s and screws (step 3, page 226) for reinforcement.

(continued next page)

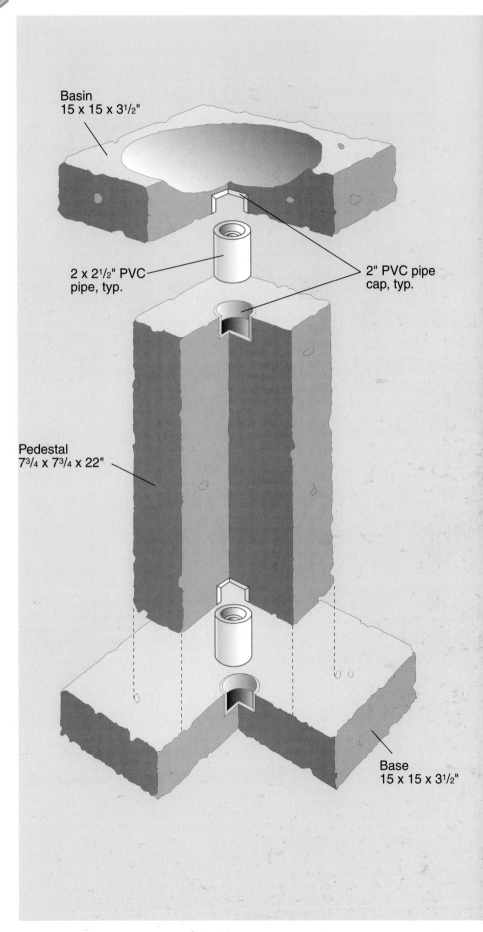

Basin
15 x 15 x 3½"

2 x 2½" PVC pipe, typ.

2" PVC pipe cap, typ.

Pedestal
7¾ x 7¾ x 22"

Base
15 x 15 x 3½"

2 Mark the center of the base form, then place a pipe cap over the center point, open side down. Mix hypertufa (pages 96 to 97). Pack it into the form, then tamp it down, using a 2 × 4. Continue tamping and packing until the hypertufa is level with the top of the form. Rap the surface with the 2 × 4 to remove air bubbles, then smooth the top with a trowel. Cover with plastic so the hypertufa can cure (page 97).

3 Center a PVC pipe cap over the bottom of the pedestal form and press the pipe cap into the form (diagram, page 225). Pack hypertufa into the form (covering the pipe cap) until it is nearly level with the top of the form, then press a pipe cap into the hypertufa. Finish filling, tamping, and smoothing as in step 2. Cover with plastic sheeting.

4 Mark the center on the bottom of the basin form, and press in a PVC pipe cap, centered over the mark. Pack a 2" layer of hypertufa into the form. Coat a shallow, gently sloped plastic bowl with vegetable oil or commercial release agent, and press it into the hypertufa to form a well. Pack and tamp the hypertufa around the bowl to form a smooth surface flush with the top of the form. Once the hypertufa sets, remove the bowl, cover the basin with plastic, and let it cure.

5 Remove the birdbath pieces from the forms, then insert a 2½"-long piece of 2" PVC pipe into the cap at the center of the base and connect it to the pipe cap in the bottom of the pedestal. Insert another 2½" length of PVC pipe into the cap at the top of the pedestal and connect it to the cap at the bottom of the basin. For a weathered look, distress the pieces, using a hammer and chisel. Knock off corners and remove any sharp edges.

Your planter can capture the rustic beauty of an antique trough or dress up a brick entryway. This hypertufa planter is easy to make and can be built to the dimensions of your choice. The brick planter (pages 230 to 231) is designed to match the brick-paver landing project (pages 143 to 145).

Building Planters with Hypertufa or Brick

You have probably seen stone troughs used as yard decorations, brimming with flowers or planted as rock gardens. These troughs, especially when covered with moss, add a touch of elegance to a lawn or garden. You can build your own trough with hypertufa and capture these rustic qualities.

Hypertufa planters last a long time and can be fashioned to resemble aged stone sinks or streamlined modern boxes, depending on your

tastes. One key is a long cure time, for maximum strength and durability (page 97).

For a more formal look, brick is the masonry material of choice. It also complements a brick-paver landing (pages 143 to 145). For a foundation for the planter, pour a slab that is separated from adjacent structures, such as a landing or house foundation, by isolation joints (step 2, page 230).

How to Build a Hypertufa Planter

Everything You Need:

Tools: Tape measure, jig saw, straightedge, drill, hacksaw, wheelbarrow, hammer, paint scraper, wire brush, propane torch, bucket.

Materials: 2"-thick polystyrene insulation board, gaffer's tape, 3½" deck screws, 4"-dia. PVC pipe, portland cement, peat moss, perlite, fiberglass fibers, concrete tint.

Form Dimensions

Outer Shell: 32 × 22" (1 for floor), 32 × 11" (2 for sides), 18 × 11" (2 for ends)

Inside Walls: 24 × 7" (2 for sides), 10 × 7" (3 for ends and center support).

1 Measure, mark, and cut pieces for the outer shell and forms, using a straightedge and a jig saw. To construct the outer form, fit end pieces inside the two side pieces and fasten the joints, using two 3½" deck screws. Reinforce each joint with gaffer's tape. Set the floor piece squarely on top of the resulting rectangle and fasten it securely in place, using screws and tape. Construct the inner form, using the same method. Cut two 2" pieces of 4" PVC pipe and set them aside.

2 Mix the hypertufa (pages 96 to 97). Center the pieces of PVC pipe in the floor of the outside shell form to establish drainage holes. Pack hypertufa firmly onto the floor of the form and around the PVC. Pack in more hypertufa to form a solid, level, 2"-thick floor.

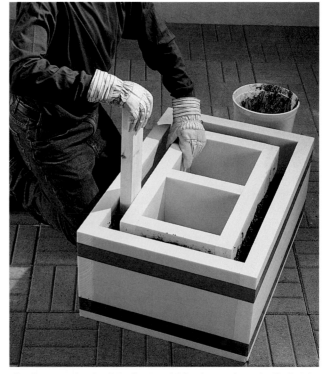

3 Center the inside form within the outer shell. Add hypertufa between the two forms and tamp it down to form the walls of the planter. Tamp the hypertufa evenly. Add hypertufa, then tamp it so it is flush with the top of the forms. Smooth the surface, using a trowel.

4 Cover the planter with sheet plastic or a tarp and let it dry for at least 48 hours. If the weather is exceptionally warm, remove the plastic and mist the planter with water occasionally during the drying process. Remove the outer form. If the walls appear dry enough to handle without damaging the planter, carefully pull apart and remove the inside form. Otherwise, let the planter dry for 24 hours more. At this point, the planter's surface will be covered with fiberglass hairs.

5 To enhance the rustic look, round the edges and corners of the planter with a hammer, then gouge it with a paint scraper or screwdriver. Brush the entire planter with a wire brush. Cure the planter, and rinse it with vinegar (page 97) to reduce the hypertufa's alkalinity and protect plants. Once the planter is completely dry, use a propane torch to burn off any fiberglass hairs. Move the torch quickly, holding it in each spot no more than a second or two. If pockets of moisture remain, they can get so hot that they explode, leaving pot holes in the planter.

TIP: Encouraging Moss

Moss helps hypertufa and other garden elements blend in as though they've been there forever. If you cannot wait for moss to form naturally, there are several ways to encourage its growth. These recipes work best if you place the ornaments in moist, shady locations.

- Pour buttermilk over the hypertufa, then press patches of fresh moss onto it. Mist the surface occasionally while you wait for moss to form.

- Paint the surface with water from a fish pond or water garden, which generally contains mold spores. Repeat the procedure several times over 24 hours, then brush on a solution of 2 tablespoons of white school glue dissolved in a quart of water.

- Dissolve 8 ounces of blue clay or porcelain clay in 3 cups of water. Add a cup of fish emulsion fertilizer and a cup of fresh moss. Blend the mixture thoroughly and paint it onto the ornament.

How to Build a Brick Planter

Everything You Need:

Tools: Mason's string, line level, drill, level, shovel, rake, hoe, wheelbarrow, hand tamper, rubber mallet, jointing tool, tape measure, broom, mason's trowel.

Materials: Type S mortar, bricks, screws, 1 × 4 lumber, stakes, 1 × 4 concrete step forms, pavers, compactible gravel, 3/8"-diameter copper or PVC tubing, sand, isolation board, cap bricks, landscape fabric.

1 Lay out the site (pages 36 to 39), using stakes, mason's strings, and a line level. Pour a concrete slab for a foundation. With larger projects, a frost footing often is required; check your local Building Code.

2 Excavate the building site, install forms and isolation boards, and pour a concrete base for the project (pages 39 to 41 and 56 to 59). Let the foundation cure for three days before building on it. Remove forms, then trim isolation boards so they are level with the tops of adjoining structures, like the landing shown above. Tip: Cover adjoining surfaces for protection.

3 Test-fit the first course of the project, then outline the project on the concrete surface. Dampen the surface slightly, then mix mortar and throw a mortar bed in one corner (pages 28 to 31). Begin laying bricks for the project, buttering the exposed end of each brick before setting it (pages 72 to 73).

4 Lay one section of the first course, checking the bricks frequently with a level to make sure the tops are level and even. Lay two corner *return* bricks perpendicular to the end bricks in the first section, and use a level to make sure they are even across the tops.

5 Install weep holes for drainage in the first course of bricks, on the sides farthest away from permanent structures. Cut ⅜"-diameter copper or PVC tubing about ¼" longer than the width of one brick, and set the pieces into the mortar joints between bricks, pressing them into the mortar bed so they touch the footing. Make sure mortar doesn't block the openings.

6 Finish building all sides of the first course. Lay the second course of bricks, reversing the directions of the corner bricks to create staggered vertical joints if using a running-bond pattern. Fill in brick courses to full height, building up one course at a time (pages 72 to 73). Check frequently to make sure the tops of the bricks are level and sides are plumb.

7 Install cap bricks to keep water from entering the cores of the brick and to enhance the visual effect. Set the cap bricks into a ⅜"-thick mortar bed, buttering one end of each cap brick. Let the mortar cure for one week. Before adding soil, pour a 4" to 6"-thick layer of gravel into the bottom of the planter for drainage, then line the bottom and sides of the planter with landscape fabric to prevent dirt from running into and clogging the drainage tubes.

Building a Stone Driveway Marker

Building a stone pillar is much like constructing a stone wall, with the added challenge of building four cornerstones into each small course. You'll need to choose your stones carefully, and remember to save a large, flat stone for a capstone. Or, buy a custom-cut stone or concrete cap to finish the top of the marker.

We built our pillar with rubble stone, which requires a lot of mortar because of the stones' irregular shapes. For strength and appearance, try to keep the mortar joints within ½" of one another in thickness. Where a thicker joint is unavoidable, you can dress it up by setting small pieces of stone into the tuck-pointing mortar during the finishing steps of the project. Review the techniques for working with stone (pages 80 to 89) before starting your project.

Stout dimensions and the choice of rubble stone for this driveway marker give it a rustic look. For a more stately or refined marker, use an ashlar, or trimmed stone and a more formal design.

Everything You Need:

Tools: Mortar box, hoe, mason's trowel, stone cutter's chisel and maul, mortar bag, jointing tool, pointing trowel, stiff-bristle brush.

Materials: Concrete mix, 2 × 4 lumber, 2½" and 3" deck screws, vegetable oil or commercial release agent, rubble stone, type M mortar, wood shims.

How to Build a Stone Driveway Marker

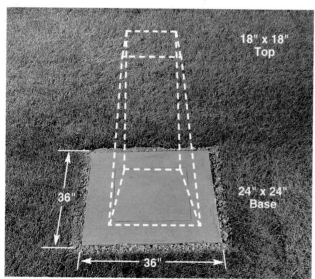

18" x 18" Top

36"

24" x 24" Base

36"

1 Pour a concrete footing that extends 6" beyond the base of the pillar on all sides (pages 56 to 59). Use the planned height of the pillar and the batter rate to calculate the size of the footing (page190). Let the footing cure for one week.

2 Sort individual stones by size and shape. Set aside suitable tie stones for use as corner stones. Use the largest stones near the bottom. Dry-lay the outside stones in the first course to get a sense of how the stones will fit together.

3 Trowel a 1"-thick bed of mortar on the footing, then lay the stones for the first course. When the outer stones are in place, fill in the center with small stones and mortar, leaving the center slightly lower than the outer stones.

4 Pack mortar between the outer stones, recessing the mortar an equal amount, roughly 1" from the faces of the stones.

5 Set each course of stone in a bed of mortar laid over the preceding course (pages 88 to 89). Stagger the vertical joints, and use a batter gauge to check slope. Place tie stones that extend into the pillar center. Use wood shims to support large stones until the mortar sets.

6 When the mortar has set enough to resist light finger pressure, smooth the joints, using a jointing tool. Keep the mortar 1" back from the stone faces. Remove the shims and fill the holes. Remove dry spattered mortar with a dry, stiff-bristle brush.

7 Lay a bed of mortar and place the capstones, then smooth the joints as in step 6. Tuck-point the pillar with a mortar bag and pointing trowel, as you would a stone wall (steps 13 to 14, page 201). Let it set up overnight. Mist regularly for one week while the mortar cures.

Building a Barbecue

The barbecue design shown here is constructed with double walls—an inner wall, made of heat-resistant fire brick set on edge, surrounding the cooking area, and an outer wall, made of engineer brick. We chose this brick because its stout dimensions mean you'll have fewer bricks to lay. You'll need to adjust the design if you select another brick size. A 4" air space between the walls helps insulate the cooking area. The walls are capped with thin pieces of cut stone.

Refractory mortar (page 29) is recommended for use with fire brick. It is heat resistant and the joints will last a long time without cracking. Ask a local brick yard to recommend a refractory mortar for outdoor use.

The foundation combines a 12"-deep footing supporting a reinforced slab. This structure, known as a floating footing, is designed to shift as a unit when temperature changes cause the ground to shift. Ask a building inspector about local Building Code specifications.

Everything You Need:

Tools: Tape measure, hammer, brickset chisel, mason's string, shovel, aviation snips, reciprocating saw or hack saw, mason's string, masonry hoe, shovel, wood float, chalk line, level, wheelbarrow, mason's trowel, jointing tool.

Materials: Garden stakes, 2 × 4 lumber, 18-gauge galvanized metal mesh, #4 rebar, 16-gauge tie wire, bolsters, fire brick (4½ × 2½ × 9"), engineer brick (4 × 3⅕ × 8"), type N mortar, refractory mortar, ⅜"-dia. dowel, metal ties, 4" tee plates, engineer brick (4 × 2 × 12"), brick sealer, stainless steel expanded mesh (23¾ × 30"), cooking grills (23⅝ × 15½"), ash pan.

A note about bricks: The brick sizes recommended below allow you to build the barbecue without splitting a lot of bricks. If the bricks recommended here are not easy to find in your area, a local brick yard can help you adjust the project dimensions to accommodate different brick sizes.

How to Pour a Floating Footing

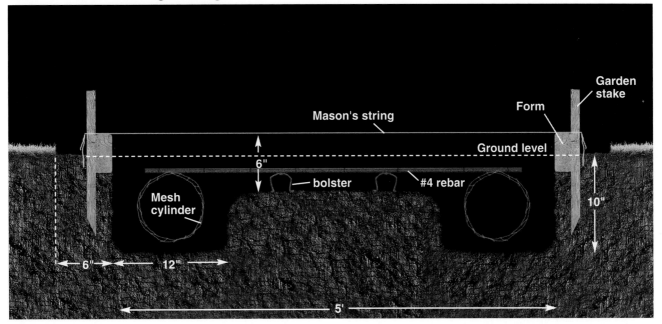

Lay out a 4 × 5 ft. area. Dig a continuous trench, 12" wide × 10" deep, along the perimeter of the area, leaving a rectangular mound in the center. Remove 4" of soil from the top of the mound, and round over the edges. Set a 2 × 4 form (page 40) around the site so that the top is 2" above the ground along the back and 1½" above the ground along the front. This slope will help shed water. Reinforce the footing with metal mesh and five 52"-long pieces of rebar. Use a mason's string and a line level to ensure that the forms are level from side to side. Roll the mesh into 6"-dia. cylinders and cut them to fit into the trench, leaving a 4" gap between the cylinder ends and the trench sides. Tie the rebar to the mesh so the outside pieces are 4" from the front and rear sides of the trench, centered from side to side. Space the remaining three bars evenly in between. Use bolsters where necessary to suspend the bar within the pour. Coat the forms with vegetable oil, and pour the concrete (pages 46 to 49).

How to Build a Barbecue

1 After the footing has cured for one week, use a chalk line to mark the layout for the inner edge of the fire brick wall. Make a line 4" in from the front edge of the footing, and a center line perpendicular to the first line. Make a 24 × 32" rectangle that starts at the 4" line and is centered on the center line.

2 Dry-lay the first course of fire brick around the outside of the rectangle, allowing for ⅛"-thick mortar joints. NOTE: Proper placement of the inner walls is necessary so they can support the grills. Start with a full brick at the 4" line to start the right and left walls. Complete the course with a cut brick in the middle of the short wall.

(continued next page)

3 Dry-lay the outer wall, as shown here, using 4 × 3⅕ × 8" nominal engineer brick. Gap the bricks for ⅜" mortar joints. The rear wall should come within ⅜" of the last fire brick in the left inner wall. Complete the left wall with a cut brick in the middle of the wall. Mark reference lines for this outer wall.

4 Make a story pole (page 191). On one side, mark eight courses of fire brick, leaving a ⅜" gap for the bottom mortar joint and ⅛" gaps for the remaining joints. The top of the final course should be 36" from the bottom edge. Transfer the top line to the other side of the pole. Lay out 11 courses of engineer brick, spacing them evenly so that the final course is flush with the 36" line. Each horizontal mortar joint will be slightly less than ½" thick.

5 Lay a bed of refractory mortar (page 29) for a ⅜" joint along the reference lines for the inner wall, then lay the first course of fire brick, using ⅛" joints between the bricks.

6 Lay the first course of the outer wall, using type N mortar (page 29). Use oiled ⅜" dowels to create weep holes behind the front bricks of the left and right walls. Alternate laying the inner and outer walls, checking your work with the story pole and a level after every other course.

7 Start the second course of the outer wall using a half brick butted against each side of the inner wall, then complete the course. Because there is a half brick in the right outer wall, you need to use two three-quarter bricks in the second course to stagger the joints.

8 Place metal ties between the corners of the inner and outer walls, at the second, third, fifth, and seventh courses. Use ties at the front junctions and along the rear walls. Mortar the joint where the left inner wall meets the rear outer wall.

9 Smooth the mortar joints with a jointing tool when the mortar has hardened enough to resist minimal finger pressure. Check the joints in both walls after every few courses. The different mortars may need smoothing at different times.

10 Add tee plates for grill supports above the fifth, sixth, and seventh courses. Use 4"-wide plates with flanges that are no more than ³⁄₃₂" thick. Position the plates along the side fire brick walls, centered 3", 12", 18", and 27" from the rear fire brick wall.

11 When both walls are complete, install the capstones. Lay a bed of type N mortar for a ⅜"-thick joint on top of the inner and outer walls. Lay the cap stone flat across the walls, keeping one end flush with the inner face of the fire brick. Make sure the bricks are level, and tool the joints when they are ready. After a week, seal the capstones and the joints between them with brick sealer and install the grills.

Before

After

Good repairs restore both the appearance and the function to failing concrete structures and surfaces. Careful work can produce a well-blended, successful repair like the one shown above.

Repairing Concrete

Concrete is one of the most durable building materials, but it still requires occasional repair and maintenance. Freezing and thawing, improper finishing techniques, a poor subbase, or lack of reinforcement all can cause problems with concrete. By addressing problems as soon as you discover them, you can prevent further damage that may be difficult or impossible to fix.

Concrete repairs fall into a wide range, from simple cleaning and sealing, to removing and replacing whole sections. Filling cracks and repairing surface damage are the most common concrete repairs.

Another effective repair is resurfacing—covering an old concrete surface with a layer of fresh concrete. It's a good solution to spalling, crazing, or popouts (page 243)—minor problems that affect the appearance more than the structure. These problems often result from inadequate preparation or incorrect finishing techniques.

As with any kind of repair, the success of the

project depends largely on good preparation and the use of the best repair products for the job. Specially formulated repair products are manufactured for just about every type of concrete repair. Be sure to read the product-use information before purchasing any products; some products need to be used in combination with others.

A good repair can outlast the rest of the structure in some cases, but if structural damage has occurred, repairing the concrete is only a temporary solution. By using the right products and techniques, however, you can make cosmetic repairs that improve the appearance of the surface and keep damage from becoming worse.

Probably the most important point to remember when repairing concrete is that curing makes repairs last longer. That means covering repaired surfaces with plastic sheeting and keeping them damp for at least a week (pages 52 to 53). In dry, hot weather, lift the plastic occasionally, and mist with water.

Concrete Repair Products

Concrete repair products include: vinyl-reinforced concrete patch (A) for filling holes, popouts, and larger cracks; hydraulic cement (B) for repairing foundations, retaining walls, and other damp areas; quick-setting cement (C) for repairing vertical surfaces and unusual shapes; anchoring cement (D) for setting hardware in concrete; concrete sealing products (E);

concrete recoating product (F) for creating a fresh surface on old concrete; masonry paint (G); joint-filler caulk (H); pour-in crack sealer (I); concrete cleaner (J); concrete fortifier (K) to strengthen concrete; bonding adhesive (L) to prepare the repair area; and concrete sand mix (M) for general repairs and resurfacing.

Tips for Disguising Repairs

Add concrete pigment to concrete patching compound to create a color that matches the original concrete. Experiment with different mixtures of pigment and repair cement until you find the right mixture. Samples should be dry to show the actual colors.

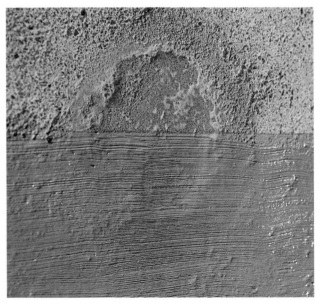

Use masonry paint to cover concrete repairs. Paint can be used on vertical or horizontal surfaces, but high-traffic surfaces will require more frequent touch-up or repainting.

Identifying Problems with Concrete

There are two general types of concrete failure: structural failure, usually resulting from outside forces like freezing water; and surface damage, most often caused by improper finishing techniques or concrete mixtures that do not have the right ratio of water to cement. Surface problems sometimes can be permanently repaired if the correct products and techniques are used. More significant damage can be patched for cosmetic purposes and to resist further damage, but the structure will eventually need to be replaced.

Common Concrete Problems

Sunken concrete is usually caused by erosion of the subbase. Some structures, like sidewalks, can be raised to repair the subbase, then relaid. A more common (and more reliable) solution is to hire a mudjacking contractor to raise the surface by injecting fresh concrete below the surface.

Frost heave is common in colder climates. Frozen ground forces concrete slabs upward, and sections of the slab can pop up. The best solution is to break off and remove the affected section or sections, repair the subbase, and pour new sections that are set off by isolation joints (page 37).

Moisture buildup occurs in concrete structures, like foundations and retaining walls, that are in constant ground contact. To identify the moisture source, tape a piece of foil to the wall. If moisture collects on the outer surface of the foil, the source likely is condensation, which can be corrected by installing a dehumidifier. If moisture is not visible on the foil, it is likely seeping through the wall. Consult a professional mason.

Staining can ruin the appearance of a concrete surface or structure. Stains can be removed with commercial-grade concrete cleaner or a variety of other chemicals (page 255). For protection against staining, seal masonry surfaces with clear sealant (pages 54 to 55).

Widespread cracks all the way through the surface, and other forms of substantial damage, are very difficult to repair effectively. If the damage to the concrete is extensive, remove and replace the structure.

Isolated cracks occur on many concrete building projects. Fill small cracks with concrete caulk or crack-filler (page 250 to 251), and patch large cracks with vinyl-reinforced patching material (pages 248 to 249).

Popouts can be caused by freezing moisture or stress, but very often they occur because the concrete surface was improperly floated or cured, causing the aggregate near the surface of the concrete to loosen. A few scattered popouts do not require attention, but if they are very large or widespread, you can repair them as you would repair holes (pages 248 to 249).

 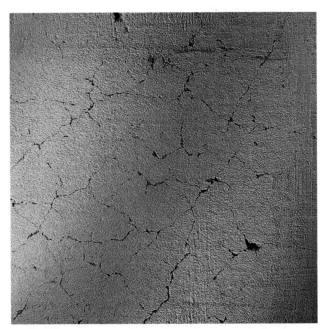

Spalling is surface deterioration of concrete. Spalling is caused by overfloating, which draws too much water to the surface, causing it to weaken and peel off over time. When spalling occurs, it is usually widespread, and the structure may need resurfacing.

Crazing is widespread hairline cracks, usually caused by overfloating or too much portland cement in the concrete. Clean and seal the surface to help prevent further crazing. For a long-term solution, resurface (pages 112 to 113).

Repairing Steps

Steps require more maintenance and repair than other concrete structures around the house because heavy use makes them more susceptible to damage. Horizontal surfaces on steps can be treated using the same products and techniques used on other masonry surfaces (pages 247 to 249). For vertical surfaces, use quick-setting cement, and shape it to fit.

Everything You Need:

Tools: Trowel, wire brush, paint brush, circular saw with masonry-cutting blade, chisel, float, edger.

Materials: Scrap lumber, vegetable oil or commercial release agent, latex bonding agent, vinyl-reinforced patching compound, quick-setting cement, plastic sheeting.

Isolated damage to step surfaces, like the deep popout being repaired above, can be fixed to renew your steps. If damage is extensive, you may need to replace the steps (pages 130 to 135).

How to Replace a Step Corner

1 Retrieve the broken corner, then clean it and the mating surface using a wire brush. Apply latex bonding agent to both surfaces. If you do not have the broken piece, you can rebuild the corner with quick-setting cement (page 246).

2 Spread a heavy layer of fortified patching compound on the surfaces to be joined, then press the broken piece into position. Lean a heavy brick or block against the repair until the patching compound sets (about 30 minutes). Cover the repair with plastic and protect it from traffic for at least one week.

How to Patch a Step Corner

1 Clean chipped concrete with a wire brush. Brush the patch area with latex bonding agent.

2 Mix patching compound with latex bonding agent, as directed by the manufacturer. Apply the mixture to the patch area, then smooth the surfaces and round the edges, as necessary, using a flexible knife or trowel.

3 Tape scrap lumber pieces around the patch as a form. Coat the insides with vegetable oil or commercial release agent so the patch won't adhere to the wood. Remove the wood when the patch is firm. Cover with plastic and protect from traffic for at least one week.

How to Patch Step Treads

1 Make a cut in the stair tread just outside the damaged area, using a circular saw with a masonry-cutting blade. Make the cut so it angles toward the back of the step. Make a horizontal cut on the riser below the damaged area, then chisel out the area in between the two cuts.

2 Cut a form board the same height as the step riser. Coat one side of the board with vegetable oil or commercial release agent to prevent it from bonding with the repair, then press it against the riser of the damaged step, and brace it in position with heavy blocks. Make sure the top of the form is flush with the top of the step tread.

3 Apply latex bonding agent to the repair area with a clean paint brush, wait until the bonding agent is tacky (no more than 30 minutes), then press a stiff mixture of quick-setting cement into the damaged area with a trowel.

4 Smooth the concrete with a float, and let it set for a few minutes. Round over the front edge of the nose with an edger. Use a trowel to slice off the sides of the patch, so it is flush with the side of the steps. Cover the repair with plastic and wait a week before allowing traffic on the repaired section.

Use hydraulic cement or quick-setting cement for repairing holes and chip-outs in vertical surfaces. Because they set up in just a few minutes, these products can be shaped to fill holes without the need for forms. If the structure is exposed constantly to moisture, use hydraulic cement.

Patching Holes

Large and small holes are treated differently when repairing concrete. The best product for filling in smaller holes (less than ½" deep) is vinyl-reinforced concrete patcher. Reinforced repair products should be applied only in layers that are ½" thick or less. For deeper holes, use sand-mix concrete with an acrylic or latex fortifier, which can be applied in layers up to 2" thick.

Patches in concrete will be more effective if you create clean, backward-angled cuts (page 250) around the damaged area, to help the repair

bond. For extensive cutting of damaged concrete, it's best to score the concrete first with a circular saw equipped with a masonry blade. Use a chisel and maul to complete the job.

TIP: You can enhance the appearance of repaired surfaces by painting repaired concrete surfaces with waterproof concrete paint once the surface has cured for at least a week. Concrete paint is formulated to resist chalking and efflorescence.

Everything You Need:

Tools: Trowels, drill with masonry-grinding disc, circular saw with masonry-cutting blade, cold chisel, hand maul, paint brush, screed board, float.

Materials: Scrap lumber, vegetable oil or commercial release agent, hydraulic cement, latex bonding agent, vinyl-reinforced patching compound, sand-mix, concrete fortifier, plastic sheeting.

How to Patch Large Areas

1 Mark straight cutting lines around the damaged area, then cut with a circular saw equipped with a masonry-cutting blade. Set the foot of the saw so the cut bevels away from the damage at a 15° angle. Chisel out any remaining concrete within the repair area. TIP: Set the foot of the saw on a thin board to protect it from the concrete.

2 Mix sand-mix concrete with concrete acrylic fortifier, and fill the damaged area slightly above the surrounding surface.

3 Smooth and feather the repair with a float until the repair is even with the surrounding surface. Recreate any surface finish, like brooming (page 52), used on the original surface. Cover the repair with plastic and protect from traffic for at least one week.

Caulking Gaps around Masonry

Cracks between a concrete walk and foundation may result in seepage, leading to a wet basement. Repair cracks with caulk-type concrete patcher.

How to Patch Small Holes

1 Cut out around the damaged area with a masonry-grinding disc mounted on a portable drill (or use a hammer and stone chisel). The cuts should bevel about 15° away from the center of the damaged area. Chisel out any loose concrete within the repair area. Always wear gloves and eye protection.

2 Apply a thin layer of latex bonding agent. The adhesive will bond with the damaged surface and create a strong bonding surface for the patching compound. Wait until the latex bonding agent is tacky (no more than 30 minutes) before proceeding to the next step.

Caulk around the mud sill, the horizontal wooden plate where the house rests on the foundation. This area should be recaulked periodically to prevent heat loss.

3 Fill the damaged area with vinyl-reinforced patching compound, applied in ¼ to ½" layers. Wait about 30 minutes between applications. Add layers of the mixture until the compound is packed to just above surface level. Feather the edges smooth, cover the repair with plastic, and protect from traffic for at least one week.

Use concrete repair caulk for quick-fix repairs to minor cracks. Although convenient, repair caulk should be viewed only as a short-term solution to improve appearance and help prevent further damage from water penetration.

Filling Cracks

The materials and methods you should use for repairing cracks in concrete depend on the location and size of the crack. For small cracks (less than ¼" wide), you can use gray-tinted concrete caulk for a quick fix. For more permanent solutions, use pourable crack filler or fortified patching cements (page 241). The patching cements are polymer compounds that significantly increase the bonding properties of cement, and also allow some flexibility. For larger cracks on horizontal surfaces, use fortified sand-mix concrete; for cracks on vertical surfaces, use hydraulic or quick-setting cement. Thorough preparation of the cracked surface is essential for creating a good bonding surface.

Everything You Need:

Tools: Wire brush, drill with wire wheel attachment, cold chisel, hand maul, paint brush, trowel.

Materials: Latex bonding agent, vinyl-reinforced patching compound, concrete caulk, sand-mix concrete, plastic sheeting.

Tips for Preparing Cracked Concrete for Repair

Clean loose material from the crack using a wire brush, or a portable drill with a wire wheel attachment. Loose material or debris left in the crack will result in a poor bond and an ineffective repair.

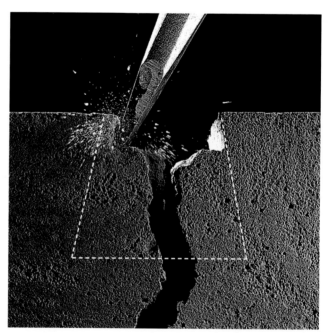

Chisel out the crack to create a backward-angled cut (wider at the base than at the surface), using a stone chisel and hammer. The angled cutout shape prevents the repair material from pushing out of the crack.

How to Repair Small Cracks

1 Prepare the crack for the repair (opposite page), then apply a thin layer of latex bonding agent to the entire repair area, using a paint brush. The latex bonding agent helps keep the repair material from loosening or popping out of the crack.

2 Mix vinyl-reinforced patching compound, and trowel it into the crack. Feather the repair with a trowel, so it is even with the surrounding surface. Cover the surface with plastic and protect it from traffic for at least a week.

Variations for Repairing Large Cracks

Sand

Shown cutaway

Horizontal surfaces: Prepare the crack (opposite page), then pour sand into the crack to within ½" of the surface. Prepare sand-mix concrete, adding a concrete fortifier, then trowel the mixture into the crack. Feather until even with the surface, using a trowel.

Vertical surfaces: Prepare the crack (opposite page). Mix vinyl-reinforced concrete or hydraulic cement, then trowel a ¼"- to ½"-thick layer into the crack until the crack is slightly overfilled. Feather the material even with the surrounding surface, then let it dry. If the crack is over ½" deep, trowel in consecutive layers. Let each layer dry before applying another.

Concrete slabs that slant toward the house can lead to foundation damage and a wet basement. Even a level slab near the foundation can cause problems. Consider asking a concrete contractor to fix it by mud-jacking, forcing wet concrete underneath the slab to lift the edge near the foundation.

Miscellaneous Concrete Repairs

There are plenty of concrete problems you may encounter around your house that are not specifically addressed in many repair manuals. These miscellaneous repairs include such tasks as patching contoured objects that have been damaged and repairing masonry veneer around the foundation of your house. You can adapt basic techniques to make just about any type of concrete repair. Remember to dampen concrete surfaces before patching so that the moisture from concrete and other patching compounds is not absorbed into the existing surface. Be sure to follow the manufacturer's directions for the repair products you use.

Everything You Need:

Tools: Putty knife, trowel, hand maul, chisel, wire brush, aviation snips, drill, soft-bristle brush.

Materials: Quick-setting cement, emery paper, wire lath, masonry anchors, concrete acrylic fortifier, sand-mix.

How to Repair Shaped Concrete

1 Scrape all loose material and debris from the damaged area, then wipe down with water. Mix quick-setting cement and trowel it into the area. Work quickly—you only have a few minutes before concrete sets up.

2 Use the trowel or a putty knife to mold the concrete to follow the form of the object being repaired. Smooth the concrete as soon as it sets up. Buff with emery paper to smooth out any ridges after the repair dries.

How to Repair Masonry Veneer

1 Chip off the crumbled, loose, or deteriorated veneer from the wall, using a cold chisel and maul. Chisel away damaged veneer until you have only good, solid surface remaining. Use care to avoid damaging the wall behind the veneer. Clean the repair area with a wire brush.

2 Clean up any metal lath in the repair area if it is in good condition. If not, cut it out with aviation snips. Add new lath where needed, using masonry anchors to hold it to the wall.

3 Mix fortified sand-mix concrete (or specialty concrete blends for wall repair), and trowel it over the lath until it is even with the surrounding surfaces.

4 Recreate the surface texture to match the surrounding area. For our project, we used a soft-bristled brush to stipple the surface. OPTION: To blend in the repair, add pigment to the sand mixture or paint the repair area after it dries (page 241).

Cleaning Poured Concrete

Our first impulse when something spills on concrete is to look for a strong cleaning agent. However, you can remove most common dirt and many stains from masonry with a strong burst of water from a pressure washer. If water alone does not do the job, try using a masonry detergent designed for use in your pressure washer. You may need to scrub stubborn stains with a stiff-bristle brush or dissolve them with an appropriate cleaning agent (chart, opposite page) As a last resort, you can clean concrete with a 5 percent solution of muriatic acid (page 23). NOTE: Muriatic acid can cause burns and may slightly alter the color of masonry surfaces. Wear protective clothing and cover any plants and wood surfaces first. Flush surfaces thoroughly with tri-sodium phosphate, then hose down the area to remove any residue.

Everything You Need:

Tools: Pressure washer, hose, stiff-bristle brush, bucket.

Materials: Recommended cleaning products, concrete sealer.

Many stains can be removed with water and a stiff-bristle brush. Consult the cleaning chart (opposite page) for specialized solvents and detergents.

Tips for Cleaning & Maintaining Concrete

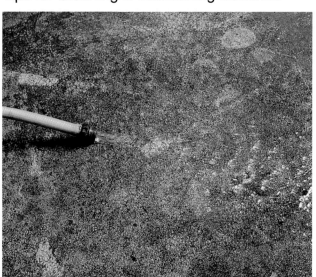

Never leave residue from a solvent or detergent on concrete. Rinse the surface with tri-sodium phosphate (TSP), then with water from a hose or a pressure washer on a *fan* setting. Allow concrete to dry for 10 days to two weeks before applying concrete sealer.

Concrete should be sealed after it cures, and once a year thereafter, or after cleanings, to prevent water from permeating and causing cracks. Apply sealer with a paint roller, squeegee, or garden sprayer.

Concrete Cleaning Products

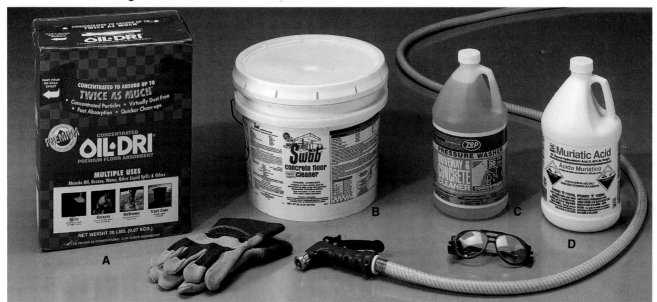

The best way to clean up spilled oil is to soak up as much of it as possible, using an oil-absorbing cleanup product (A). Once you have soaked up as much oil as you can, dispose of the oil-soaked material and clean the surface with a pressure washer and a pressure-washer-compatible detergent designed specifically for your driveway (B) or garage floor (C). These solu-

tions are designed for general cleaning. Consult the chart below for solutions to stubborn stains. Whichever product you use, follow the safety precautions on the container carefully. For very stubborn stains, a 5 percent solution of muriatic acid (D) may be effective (opposite page). Wear protective clothing and observe the precautions on the container.

Cleaning Solutions for Poured Concrete Surfaces

Stain	Solution	Stain	Solution
Asphalt, tar, or pitch	Scrape off as much as possible. Scrub with scouring powder, water, and a stiff-bristle brush.	Efflorescence (salt deposits)	Remove as much as possible with a dry brush, then rinse with a pressure washer.
Blood	Wet the area with water. Wearing gloves and a mask, cover with a thin layer of sodium peroxide powder. Mist the powder with water to keep it from blowing away. CAUTION: Peroxide is highly caustic. After several minutes, sweep up as much of the powder as possible and dispose of it, then scrub with water and a stiff-bristle brush.	Oil, oil-based products	As soon as possible, cover the area with a commercial oil-absorbent product. Portland cement, sawdust, talc, cat litter, cornmeal, and corn starch also work well. Allow the product to soak up the oil. Remove as much as possible with a shovel, then wash the surface with a pressure washer.
Caulking, chewing gum	Scrape off as much as possible. Cover with a rag soaked in denatured alcohol and plastic to slow evaporation. After the alcohol has evaporated, brush off the remaining material with a stiff-bristle brush. Wash the surface with hot water and scouring powder.	Wet paint (water-based)	Soak up paint with paper towels or rags. Scrub the area with scouring powder, water, and a stiff-bristle brush.
Coffee, tea, soft drinks, alcohol	Soak a rag in a 1-to-4 solution of glycerin and water and place it on the surface for 15 minutes. Remove and clean the surface with water and a stiff-bristle brush.	Dry paint	Brush on a small amount of paint stripper. Allow the paint stripper to loosen the paint before scrubbing off the residue with scouring powder and a stiff-bristle brush.

Choose the best materials and techniques for repairing problems with brick and block structures. A simple chip or popout, like the one shown above, can be fixed easily by packing the damaged area with latex-fortified mortar. More extensive problems require more complicated solutions.

Repairing Brick & Block Structures

Brick, block, and mortar are very durable building materials. But when they are combined in a permanent structure, stress and the forces of nature can lead to damage that requires attention. Common examples of brick and block structural problems include walls with failing mortar joints, cracked or crumbling bricks or blocks, and worn or discolored surfaces.

Many common brick and block problems can be corrected with simple repairs. These require just a few basic masonry tools (opposite page) and a minimal investment of time and money. The completed repair job will result in a dramatic im-

provement in the appearance and strength of the structure. With regular maintenance and cleaning, repaired structures will provide many years of productive use.

Brick and block are used frequently in the construction of foundation walls, retaining walls, and other load-bearing structures. Simple repairs, like filling cracks, can be done with little risk. Always get a professional evaluation from a masonry contractor before attempting major repairs to brick and block structures. Review the basic techniques for working with brick and block (pages 62 to 79) before starting your project.

Tools for Repairing Brick & Block Structures

Basic tools for repairing brick and block include: a masonry chisel (A) for cutting new brick or block, stone chisel (B) for breaking up and repairing masonry structures, raking tool (C) for cleaning mortar out of joints, mason's trowel (D) for applying mortar to concrete block, pointing trowel (E) for applying mortar to brick or block and for smoothing out fresh repairs, mason's hammer (F), ½"-wide (G) and ⅜"-wide (H) jointing tools for packing fresh mortar into joints, and tuck-pointer (I) for finishing mortar joints.

Tips for Working with Mortar

Add concrete fortifier to mortar for making repairs. Fortifier, usually acrylic or latex based, increases the mortar's strength and its ability to bond.

Add mortar tint to plain mortar so repairs blend in (page 31). Compare tint samples, available from concrete products suppliers, to match mortar colors.

Identifying Brick & Block Problems

Inspect damaged brick and block structures closely before you begin any repair work. Accurately identifying the nature and cause of the damage is an important step before choosing the best solution for the problem.

Look for obvious clues, like overgrown tree roots, or damaged gutters that let water drain onto masonry surfaces. Also check the slope of the adjacent landscape; it may need to be regraded to direct water away from a brick or block wall (see *Landscape Design & Construction,* Black & Decker Home Improvement Library™), or consult a landscape architect.

Repairs fail when the original source of the problem is not eliminated prior to making the repair. When a concrete patch separates, for example, it means that the opposing stresses causing the crack are still at work on the structure. Find and correct the cause (often a failing subbase or stress from water or freezing and thawing), then redo the repair.

Types of Brick & Block Problems

Deteriorated mortar joints are common problems in brick and block structures—mortar is softer than most bricks or blocks and is more prone to damage. Deterioration is not always visible, so probe surrounding joints with a screwdriver to see if they are sound. Tuck-point deteriorated joints (page 261).

Major structural damage, like the damage to this brick porch, usually requires removal of the existing structure, improvements to the subbase, and reconstruction of the structure. Projects of this nature should only be attempted by professional masons.

Damage to concrete blocks often results from repeated freezing and thawing of moisture trapped in the wall or in the blocks themselves. Instead of replacing the whole block, chip out the face of the block and replacing it with a concrete paver with the same dimensions as the face of the block (pages 264 to 265).

Spalling occurs when freezing water or other forces cause enough directional pressure to fracture a brick. The best solution is to replace the entire brick (pages 262 to 263) while eliminating the source of the pressure, if possible. Spalled blocks can be refaced (previous photo). TIP: Chip off a piece of the damaged brick to use as a color reference when looking for a replacement.

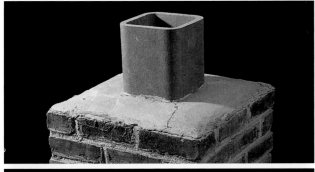

Damaged mortar caps on chimneys allow water into the flue area, where it can damage the chimney and even the roof or interior walls. Small-scale damage (top photo) can be patched with fire-rated silicone caulk. If damage is extensive (bottom photo), repair or replace the mortar cap (page 271).

Stains and discoloration can be caused by external sources or by minerals leeching to the surface from within the brick or block (called efflorescence). If the stain does not wash away easily with water, use a cleaning solution (page 255).

Before   After

Make timely repairs to brick and block structures. Tuck-pointing deteriorated mortar joints is a common repair that, like other types of repair, improves the appearance of the structure or surface and helps prevent further damage.

Repairing Brick & Block Walls

The most common brick and block wall repair is tuck-pointing, the process of replacing failed mortar joints with fresh mortar. Tuck-pointing is a highly useful repair technique for any homeowner. It can be used to repair walls, chimneys, brick veneer, or any other structure where the bricks or blocks are bonded with mortar.

Minor cosmetic repairs can be attempted on any type of wall, from free-standing garden walls to block foundations. Filling minor cracks with caulk or repair compound, and patching popouts or chips are good examples of minor repairs. Consult a professional before attempting any major repairs, like replacing brick or blocks, or rebuilding a structure—especially if you are dealing with a load-bearing structure.

Basement walls are a frequent trouble area for homeowners. Constant moisture and stress created by ground contact can cause leaks, bowing, and paint failure. Small leaks and cracks can be patched with hydraulic cement.

Masonry-based waterproofing products can be applied to give deteriorated walls a fresh appearance. Persistent moisture problems are most often caused by improper grading of soil around the foundation or a malfunctioning downspout and gutter system.

NOTE: The repairs shown in this section feature brick and block walls. The same techniques may be used for other brick and block structures.

Everything You Need:

Tools: Raking tool, mortar hawk, tuck-pointer, jointing tool, bricklayer's hammer, mason's trowel, mason's or stone chisel, pointing trowel, drill with masonry disc and bit, stiff-bristle brush.

Materials: Mortar, gravel, scrap of metal flashing, concrete fortifier, replacement bricks or blocks.

How to Tuck-point Mortar Joints

1 Clean out loose or deteriorated mortar to a depth of ¼" to ¾". Use a mortar raking tool (top) first, then switch to a masonry chisel and a hammer (bottom) if the mortar is stubborn. Clear away all loose debris, and dampen the surface with water before applying fresh mortar.

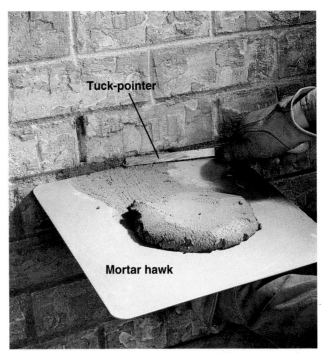

Tuck-pointer

Mortar hawk

2 Mix the mortar, adding concrete fortifier; add tint if necessary (pages 31 and 257). Load mortar onto a mortar hawk, then push it into the horizontal joints with a tuck-pointer. Apply mortar in ¼"-thick layers, and let each layer dry for 30 minutes before applying another. Fill the joints until the mortar is flush with the face of the brick or block.

3 Apply the first layer of mortar into the vertical joints by scooping mortar onto the back of a tuck-pointer, and pressing it into the joint. Work from the top downward.

4 After the final layer of mortar is applied, smooth the joints with a jointing tool that matches the profile of the old mortar joints. Tool the horizontal joints first. Let the mortar dry until it is crumbly, then brush off the excess mortar with a stiff-bristle brush.

How to Replace a Damaged Brick

1 Score the damaged brick so it will break apart more easily for removal: use a drill with a masonry-cutting disc to score lines along the surface of the brick and in the mortar joints surrounding the brick.

2 Use a mason's chisel and hammer to break apart the damaged brick along the scored lines. Rap sharply on the chisel with the hammer, being careful not to damage surrounding bricks. TIP: Save fragments to use as a color reference when you shop for replacement bricks.

3 Chisel out any remaining mortar in the cavity, then brush out debris with a stiff-bristle or wire brush to create a clean surface for the new mortar. Rinse the surface of the repair area with water.

4 Mix the mortar for the repair (pages 28 to 31), adding concrete fortifier to the mixture, and tint if needed to match old mortar (pages 31 and 257). Use a pointing trowel to apply a 1"-thick layer of mortar at the bottom and sides of the cavity.

5 Dampen the replacement brick slightly, then apply mortar to the ends and top of the brick. Fit the brick into the cavity and rap it with the handle of the trowel until the face is flush with the surrounding bricks. If needed, press additional mortar into the joints with a pointing trowel.

6 Scrape away excess mortar with a masonry trowel, then smooth the joints with a jointing tool that matches the profile of the surrounding mortar joints. Let the mortar set until crumbly, then brush the joints to remove excess mortar.

Tips for Removing & Replacing Several Bricks

For walls with extensive damage, remove bricks from the top down, one row at a time, until the entire damaged area is removed. Replace bricks using the techniques shown above and in the section on building with brick and block (pages 62 to 79). CAUTION: Do not dismantle load-bearing brick structures like foundation walls—consult a professional mason for these repairs.

For walls with internal damaged areas, remove only the damaged section, keeping the upper layers intact if they are in good condition. Do not remove more than four adjacent bricks in one area—if the damaged area is larger, it will require temporary support, which is a job for a professional mason.

How to Reface a Damaged Concrete Block

Cores (hollow)

1 Drill several holes into the face of the deteriorated block at the cores (hollow spots) of the block (page 68) using a drill and masonry bit. Wear protective eye covering when drilling or breaking apart concrete.

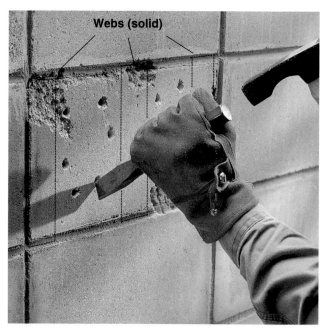

Webs (solid)

2 Using the holes as starting points, chip away the face of the block over the core areas, using a chisel and hammer. Be careful to avoid damaging surrounding blocks and try to leave the block face intact in front of the solid web areas.

3 Use a stone chisel to carefully chip out a 2"-deep recess in the web areas. Mark and score cutting lines 2" back from the block face, then chisel away the block in the recess area. Avoid deepening the recess more than 2" because the remaining web sections provide a bonding surface for the concrete paver that will be installed to replace the face of the concrete block.

4 Mix mortar (pages 28 to 31 and 257), then apply a 1"-thick layer to the sides and bottom of the opening, to the webs, and to the top edge and web locations on the paver (use an 8 × 16" paver to fit standard blocks). Press the paver into the cavity, flush with the surrounding blocks. Add mortar to the joints if needed, then prop a 2 × 4 against the paver until the mortar sets. Finish the joints with a jointing tool.

How to Reinforce a Section of Refaced Blocks

1 Reinforce repair areas spanning two or more adjacent block faces. Start by drilling a few holes in a small area over a core in the block located directly above the repair area. Chip out the block face between the holes with a cold chisel.

2 Prepare a thin mortar mix made from 1 part gravel and 2 parts dry mortar, then add water. The mixture should be thin enough to pour easily, but not soupy. NOTE: Adding small amounts of gravel increases the strength of the mortar and increases the yield of the batch.

3 Pour the mortar/gravel mixture into the hole above the repair area, using a piece of metal flashing as a funnel. Continue mixing and filling the hole until it will not accept any more mortar. The mortar will dry to form a reinforcing column that is bonded to the backs of the pavers used to reface the blocks.

4 Patch the hole above the repair area by using a pointing trowel to fill the hole with plain mortar mix. Smooth the surface with the pointing trowel. When the mortar resists finger pressure, finish the joint below the patch with a jointing tool.

Cleaning & Painting Brick & Block

Use a pressure washer to clean large brick and block structures. Pressure washers can be rented from most rental centers. Be sure to obtain detailed operating and safety instructions from the rental agent.

Solvent Solutions for Common Brick & Block Stains

• **Egg splatter:** Dissolve oxalic acid crystals in water, following manufacturer's instructions, in a nonmetallic container. Brush onto the surface.

• **Efflorescence:** Scrub surface with a stiff-bristled brush. Use a household cleaning solution for surfaces with heavy accumulation.

• **Iron stains:** Spray or brush a solution of oxalic acid crystals dissolved in water, following manufacturer's instructions. Apply directly to the stain.

• **Ivy:** Cut vines away from the surface (do not pull them off). Let remaining stems dry up, then scrub them off with a stiff-bristled brush and household cleaning solution.

• **Oil:** Apply a paste made of mineral spirits and an inert material like sawdust.

• **Paint stains:** Remove new paint with a solution of tri-sodium phosphate (TSP) and water, following manufacturer's mixing instructions. Old paint can usually be removed with heavy scrubbing or sandblasting.

• **Plant growth:** Use weed killer according to manufacturer's directions.

• **Smoke stains:** Scrub surface with household cleanser containing bleach, or use a mixture of ammonia and water.

Check brick and block surfaces annually and remove stains or discoloration. Most problems are easy to correct if they are treated in a timely fashion. Regular maintenance will help brick and block structures remain attractive and durable for a long time. Refer to the information below for cleaning tips that address specific staining problems.

Painted brick and block structures can be spruced up by applying a fresh coat of paint. As with any other painting job, thorough surface preparation and a quality primer are critical to a successful outcome.

Many stains can be removed easily, using a commercial brick and block detergent, available at home centers, but remember:

• Always test cleaning solutions on a small inconspicuous part of the surface and evaluate the results.

• Some chemicals and their fumes may be harmful. Be sure to follow manufacturer's safety and use recommendations. Wear protective clothing.

• Soak the surface to be cleaned with water before you apply any solutions. This keeps solutions from soaking in too quickly. Rinse the surface thoroughly after cleaning to wash off any remaining cleaning solution.

Tips for Cleaning Brick & Block Surfaces

Mix a paste made from cleaning solvents (chart, opposite page) and talcum or flour. Apply paste directly to stain, let it dry, then scrape it off with a vinyl or plastic scraper.

Use a nylon scraper or a thin block of wood to remove spilled mortar that has hardened. Avoid using metal scrapers, which can damage masonry surfaces.

Mask off windows, siding, decorative millwork, and other exposed nonmasonry surfaces before cleaning brick and block. Careful masking is essential if you are using harsh cleaning chemicals, such as muriatic acid.

Tips for Painting Masonry

Clean mortar joints, using a drill with a wire wheel attachment before applying paint. Scrub off loose paint, dirt, mildew, and mineral deposits so the paint will bond better.

Apply masonry primer before repainting brick or block walls. Primer helps eliminate stains and prevent problems such as efflorescence.

Ninety-five percent of wet basement problems occur because water pools near the foundation. The cause is usually failing roof gutters and downspouts or an improperly graded yard. The soil around your house should slope away from the foundation at a rate of ¾" per foot. Before tackling symptoms such as wet basement walls, it's important to repair moisture problems at their source.

Protecting Basement Walls

Failing gutters, broken or leaking pipes, condensation, and seepage are the most common causes of basement moisture. If allowed to persist, dampness can cause major damage to concrete basement walls. There are several effective ways to seal and protect the walls. If condensation is the source of the problem, check first that your clothes dryer is properly vented, and install a dehumidifier. If water is seeping in through small cracks or holes in the walls, repair damaged gutters and leaky pipes, and check the grade of the soil around your foundation. Once you've addressed the problem at its source, create a water-proof seal over openings in the basement walls. To stop occasional seepage, coat the walls with masonry sealer. For more frequent seepage, seal the openings and resurface the walls with a water-resistant masonry coating. Heavy-duty coatings, such as surface bonding cement (opposite page) are best for very damp conditions. Thinner brush-on coatings are also available. For chronic seepage, ask a contractor to install a baseboard gutter and drain system. REMEMBER: To prevent long-term damage, it's necessary to identify the source of the moisture and make repairs both inside and outside your home, so moisture no longer penetrates foundation walls.

Everything You Need:

Tools: Wire brush, heavy-duty stirrer, stiff-bristle paintbrush, sponge, square-end trowel, scratching tool.

Materials: Household cleaner, waterproof masonry sealer, water-resistant masonry coating, aluminum foil, duct tape.

Tips for Inspecting & Sealing Basement Walls

Paint that is peeling off basement walls usually indicates water seepage from outside that is trapped between the walls and the paint.

Tape a square of aluminum foil to a masonry wall to identify high moisture levels. Check the foil after 24 hours. Beads of water on top of the foil indicate high humidity in the room. Beads of water underneath suggest water seepage through the wall from outside.

To control minor seepage through porous masonry, seal walls with a masonry sealer. Clean the walls and prepare the sealer, according to manufacturer's instructions. Apply sealer to the walls, including all masonry joints.

How to Damp-proof Masonry Walls

1 Resurface heavily cracked masonry walls with a water-resistant masonry coating, such as surface bonding cement. Clean and dampen the walls, according to the coating manufacturer's instructions, then fill large cracks and holes with the coating. Finally, plaster a ¼" layer of the coating on the walls, using a square-end trowel. Specially formulated heavy-duty masonry coatings are available for very damp conditions.

2 Let the coating set up for several hours, then scratch the surface with a paint roller cleaner or a homemade scratching tool (page 221). After 24 hours, apply a second, smooth coat. Mist the wall twice a day for three days as the coating cures.

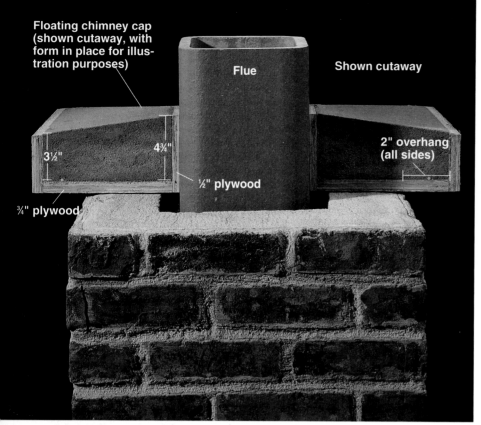

Floating chimney cap (shown cutaway, with form in place for illustration purposes)

Flue

Shown cutaway

¾" plywood

3½"

4¾"

½" plywood

2" overhang (all sides)

Repairing & Replacing Chimney Caps

Chimney caps undergo stress because the temperatures of the cap and chimney flue fluctuate dramatically. Use fire-rated silicone caulk to patch minor cracks. For more extensive repairs, reapply fresh mortar over the cap, or replace the old cap for a permanent solution.

Everything You Need:

Tools: Hammer, stone chisel, wire brush, drill, float, pointing trowel, tape measure, caulk gun.

Materials: Mortar, concrete fortifier, ½" and ¾" plywood, ¼" dowel, 1½" wood screws, vegetable oil or a commercial release agent, fire-rated silicone caulk, fire-rated rope or mineral wool.

A chimney cap expands and shrinks as temperatures change inside and outside the chimney. This often results in cracking and annual treks up to the roof for repairs. A floating chimney cap (above) is cast in a form, using mortar or sand-mix concrete, then placed on the top of the chimney (opposite page). You can repair a damaged cap by chipping off the deteriorated sections and adding fresh mortar (below).

How to Repair a Chimney Cap

1 Carefully break apart and remove the deteriorated sections of the chimney cap, using a stone chisel and hammer. Be very careful when chiseling around the flue.

2 Mix a batch of latex-fortified mortar (pages 28 to 31 and 257). Trowel an even layer of mortar all the way around the chimney cap, following the slope of the existing cap. Mortar should cover the chimney from the outside edges of the chimney bricks to the flue. Smooth out the mortar with a wood float, trying to recreate the original slope of the chimney cap. Inspect mortar annually.

How to Cast & Install a Replacement Chimney Cap

1 Measure the chimney and the chimney flue and build a form from ½" and ¾" plywood (form dimensions on opposite page, top). Attach the form to a plywood base, using 1½" wood screws to connect all form parts. Glue ⅜" dowels to the base, 1" inside the form. The dowels will cast a drip edge into the cap. Coat the inside of the form with vegetable oil or a commercial release agent.

2 Prepare a stiff (dry) mixture of mortar (pages 28 to 31) to cast the cap—for average-sized chimneys, two 60-lb. bags of dry mix should yield enough mortar. Fill the form with mortar. Rest a wood float across the edges of the form, and smooth the mortar. Keep angles sharp at the corners. Let the cap cure for at least a week, then carefully disassemble the form.

3 Chip off the old mortar cap completely, and clean the top of the chimney with a wire brush. With a helper, transport the chimney cap onto the roof and set it directly onto the chimney, centered so the overhang is equal on all sides. (See pages 22 to 23 for tips on working safely at heights.) For the new cap to function properly, do not bond it to the chimney or the flue.

4 Shift the cap so the gap next to the flue is even on all sides, then fill in the gap with fire-rated rope or mineral wool. Caulk over the fill material with a very heavy bead of fire-rated silicone caulk. Also caulk the joint at the underside of the cap. Inspect caulk every other year, and refresh as needed.

A masonry fireplace is a treasured feature in many homes. Most fireplaces are constructed with several different materials, including two or more types of brick and mortar, concrete, concrete block, metal, and fireclay. Routine maintenance is essential to the efficiency and longevity of your fireplace, as well as to the safety of your home.

Repairing a Firebox

Masonry fireplaces are built according to strict specifications designed to maximize heating efficiency, smoke exhaustion, and above all, safety. The internal chamber where the fire burns, known as the *firebox*, is made with heat-resistant firebrick and a special mortar that can withstand extremely high temperatures. For added heat resistance, mortar joints in firebrick construction are smaller than with other types of brick, usually ¹⁄₁₆" to ¼" thick.

The firebox reflects the fire's heat into the room, and it insulates the surrounding structure from the high temperatures that can cause damage. Therefore, in addition to having your fireplace and chimney inspected and cleaned regularly, it's a good idea to check the firebox for crumbling mortar joints and loose, cracked, or chipped bricks.

Signs of severe damage or wear in the firebox may indicate serious problems elsewhere in the fireplace or chimney and should be reported to a professional. But you can fix most minor problems yourself, provided you use only materials rated for fireplaces. Some refractory mortars are sold premixed so it is not necessary to add water. Whichever product you select, make sure it is rated for use with fire brick.

Everything You Need:

Tools: Shop light, mirror, flashlight, stiff-bristle brush, sponge, screwdriver, masonry or stone chisel, mason's trowel, jointing tool.

Materials: Fireplace cleaner, firebrick, refractory mortar.

How to Inspect & Repair a Firebox

1 Begin your inspection by cleaning the fireplace thoroughly. If the bricks and mortar joints are not clearly visible, use a fireplace cleaner and a stiff-bristle brush to remove the soot and creosote buildup. Use a shop light and mirror to view the upper areas of the firebox and the damper opening.

2 Using a flashlight, inspect the bricks and mortar in the firebox. Check for loose mortar by lightly scraping the joints with a screwdriver. Look for cracks and feel around for any loose bricks.

3 Remove any loose or damaged bricks, and scrape off the old mortar, using a masonry or stone chisel. Clean the edges of the surrounding brick with a stiff-bristle brush. If you need replacement bricks, bring an original one to a fireplace or brick supplier to be sure you get a perfect match.

4 Apply refractory mortar (page 29) to the new bricks, following the mortar manufacturer's directions. Gently slide the bricks into place until they are flush with the surrounding bricks. Scrape off excess mortar with a trowel. Use a jointing tool to tool the mortar joints.

Repairing Stonework

Damage to stonework is typically caused by frost heave, erosion or deterioration of mortar, or by stones that have worked out of place. Dry-stone walls are more susceptible to erosion and popping, while mortared walls develop cracks that admit water, which can freeze and cause further damage.

Inspect stone structures once a year for signs of damage and deterioration. Replacing a stone or repointing crumbling mortar now will save you a lot of work in the long run.

A leaning stone column or wall probably suffers from erosion or foundation problems, and can be dangerous if neglected. If you have the time, you can tear down and rebuild dry-laid structures, but mortared structures with excessive lean need professional help.

Everything You Need:

Tools: Maul, chisel, camera, shovel, hand tamper, level, batter gauge, stiff-bristle brush, trowels for mixing and pointing, mortar bag, masonry chisels.

Materials: Wood shims, carpet-covered 2 × 4, chalk, compactible gravel, replacement stones, type M mortar, mortar tint.

Stones in a wall can become dislodged due to soil settling, erosion, or seasonal freeze-thaw cycles. Make the necessary repairs before the problem migrates to other areas.

Tips for Replacing Popped Stones

Return a popped stone to its original position. If other stones have settled in its place, drive shims between neighboring stones to make room for the popped stone. Be careful not to wedge too far.

Use a 2 × 4 covered with carpet to avoid damaging the stone when hammering it into place. After hammering, make sure a replacement stone hasn't damaged or dislodged the adjoining stones.

How to Rebuild a Dry-stone Wall Section

1 Before you start, study the wall and determine how much of it needs to be rebuilt. Plan to dismantle the wall in a "V" shape, centered on the damaged section. Number each stone and mark its orientation with chalk so you can rebuild it following the original design. TIP: Photograph the wall, making sure the markings are visible.

2 Capstones are often set in a mortar bed atop the last course of stone. You may need to chip out the mortar with a maul and chisel to remove the capstones. Remove the marked stones, taking care to check the overall stability of the wall as you work.

3 Rebuild the wall, one course at a time, using replacement stones only when necessary. Start each course at the ends and work toward the center. On thick walls, set the face stones first, then fill in the center with smaller stones (pages 188 to 189). Check your work with a level, and use a batter gauge to maintain the batter of the wall (page 89). If your capstones were mortared, re-lay them in fresh mortar. Wash off the chalk with water and a stiff-bristle brush.

Tip: If you're rebuilding because of erosion, dig a trench at least 6" deep under the damaged area, and fill it with compactible gravel. Tamp the gravel with a hand tamper. This will improve drainage and prevent water from washing soil out from beneath the wall.

Tips for Repairing Mortared Stone Walls

Tint mortar for repair work so it blends with the existing mortar (page 31). Mix several samples of mortar, adding a different amount of tint to each, and allow them to dry thoroughly. Compare each sample to the old mortar, and choose the closest match.

Use a mortar bag to restore weathered and damaged mortar joints over an entire structure. Remove loose mortar (see below) and clean all surfaces with a stiff-bristle brush and water. Dampen the joints before tuck-pointing, and cover all of the joints, smoothing and brushing as necessary (pages 88 to 89).

How to Repoint Mortar Joints

1 Carefully rake out cracked and crumbling mortar, stopping when you reach solid mortar. Remove loose mortar and debris with a stiff-bristle brush. TIP: Rake the joints with a chisel and maul, or make your own raking tool by placing an old screwdriver in a vice and bending the shaft about 45°.

2 Mix type M mortar (page 29), then dampen the repair surfaces with clean water. Working from the top down, pack mortar into the crevices, using a pointing trowel. Smooth the mortar when it has set up enough to resist light finger pressure. Remove excess mortar with a stiff-bristle brush.

How to Replace a Stone in a Mortared Wall

1 Remove the damaged stone by chiseling out the surrounding mortar, using a masonry chisel or a modified screwdriver (opposite page). Drive the chisel toward the damaged stone to avoid harming neighboring stones. Once the stone is out, chisel the surfaces inside the cavity as smooth as possible.

2 Brush out the cavity to remove loose mortar and debris. Test the surrounding mortar, and chisel or scrape out any mortar that isn't firmly bonded.

3 Dry-fit the replacement stone. The stone should be stable in the cavity and blend with the rest of the wall. You can mark the stone with chalk and cut it to fit (page 86 to 87), but excessive cutting will result in a conspicuous repair.

4 Mist the stone and cavity lightly, then apply type M mortar around the inside of the cavity, using a trowel. Butter all mating sides of the replacement stone. Insert the stone and wiggle it forcefully to remove any air pockets. Use a pointing trowel to pack the mortar solidly around the stone. Smooth the mortar when it has set up (step 2, opposite page).

Repairing Stucco

Harsh weather can cause stucco to crack and crumble. You can repair small areas with premixed stucco repair compound. For repairs more than 4" in diameter, start with dry stucco mix and water. The project on the opposite page tells you how to patch a large area, including replacing the underlying building paper and lath to create a gripping surface for the new stucco.

Everything You Need:

Tools: Caulk gun, masonry chisel, maul, wire brush, putty knife, mason's trowel, square-end trowel, hammer, whisk broom, circular saw with masonry-cutting blade, chisel, aviation snips, pry bar, scratching tool.

Materials: Metal primer, stucco patching compound, stucco mix, 1½" roofing nails, 15-lb. building paper, self-furring metal lath, masonry caulk, tint.

Fill thin cracks with masonry caulk. Overfill the crack with caulk, and feather until it is flush with the stucco. Allow the caulk to set, then paint to match. Masonry caulk stays semiflexible, preventing further cracking.

How to Patch Small Areas

1 Clean out loose material from the repair area with a wire brush. Remove rust from any exposed metal lath, and treat the lath with metal primer.

2 Trowel premixed stucco repair compound into the repair area with a putty knife or pointed trowel, overfilling slightly. (Read manufacturer's directions—drying times and application technique may vary.)

3 Smooth the repair with a putty knife or trowel, feathering it even with the surrounding surface. Use a whisk broom or trowel to create a matching texture, then paint the area with masonry paint.

How to Patch Large Areas

1 Mark a square around the damaged area. Cut out the square, using a circular saw with a masonry-cutting blade. Start with the blade set to an ⅛" depth and make several passes, increasing the blade's setting until it cuts through the lath, producing sparks. Remove the stucco, building paper, and lath, using a chisel, maul, aviation snips, and pry bar, then attach new paper and lath (pages 92 to 93) as a foundation for new stucco.

2 Apply a ⅜" scratch coat of stucco to the new lath (page 220 to 221). Scratch the surface with a scratching tool. Mist the stucco with water twice a day for two days to assist curing.

3 Mix and apply the brown coat, also ⅜" thick (page 220 to 221). Let the brown coat cure for two days. While it cures, mist the coat with water several times.

4 Dampen the wall, then apply the tinted finish coat to match the old stucco (page 95). The finish coat above was *dashed* on with the flick of a whisk broom, then flattened with a trowel. Keep the finish coat damp for a week while it cures.

Converting Measurements

To Convert:	To:	Multiply by:
Inches	Millimeters	25.4
Inches	Centimeters	2.54
Feet	Meters	0.305
Yards	Meters	0.914
Square inches	Square centimeters	6.45
Square feet	Square meters	0.093
Square yards	Square meters	0.836
Cubic inches	Cubic centimeters	16.4
Cubic feet	Cubic meters	0.0283
Cubic yards	Cubic meters	0.765
Ounces	Milliliters	30.0
Pints (U.S.)	Liters	0.473 (Imp. 0.568)
Quarts (U.S.)	Liters	0.946 (Imp. 1.136)
Gallons (U.S.)	Liters	3.785 (Imp. 4.546)
Ounces	Grams	28.4
Pounds	Kilograms	0.454

To Convert:	To:	Multiply by:
Millimeters	Inches	0.039
Centimeters	Inches	0.394
Meters	Feet	3.28
Meters	Yards	1.09
Square centimeters	Square inches	0.155
Square meters	Square feet	10.8
Square meters	Square yards	1.2
Cubic centimeters	Cubic inches	0.061
Cubic meters	Cubic feet	35.3
Cubic meters	Cubic yards	1.31
Milliliters	Ounces	.033
Liters	Pints (U.S.)	2.114 (Imp. 1.76)
Liters	Quarts (U.S.)	1.057 (Imp. 0.88)
Liters	Gallons (U.S.)	0.264 (Imp. 0.22)
Grams	Ounces	0.035
Kilograms	Pounds	2.2

Lumber Dimensions

Nominal - U.S.	Actual - U.S.	METRIC
1 × 2	¾ × 1½"	19 × 38 mm
1 × 3	¾ × 2½"	19 × 64 mm
1 × 4	¾ × 3½"	19 × 89 mm
1 × 5	¾ × 4½"	19 × 114 mm
1 × 6	¾ × 5½"	19 × 140 mm
1 × 7	¾ × 6¼"	19 × 159 mm
1 × 8	¾ × 7¼"	19 × 184 mm
1 × 10	¾ × 9¼"	19 × 235 mm
1 × 12	¾ × 11¼"	19 × 286 mm
1¼ × 4	1 × 3½"	25 × 89 mm
1¼ × 6	1 × 5½"	25 × 140 mm
1¼ × 8	1 × 7¼"	25 × 184 mm
1¼ × 10	1 × 9¼"	25 × 235 mm
1¼ × 12	1 × 11¼"	25 × 286 mm
1½ × 4	1¼ × 3½"	32 × 89 mm
1½ × 6	1¼ × 5½"	32 × 140 mm
1½ × 8	1¼ × 7¼"	32 × 184 mm
1½ × 10	1¼ × 9¼"	32 × 235 mm
1½ × 12	1¼ × 11¼"	32 × 286 mm
2 × 4	1½ × 3½"	38 × 89 mm
2 × 6	1½ × 5½"	38 × 140 mm
2 × 8	1½ × 7¼"	38 × 184 mm
2 × 10	1½ × 9¼"	38 × 235 mm
2 × 12	1½ × 11¼"	38 × 286 mm
3 × 6	2½ × 5½"	64 × 140 mm
4 × 4	3½ × 3½"	89 × 89 mm
4 × 6	3½ × 5½"	89 × 140 mm

Liquid Measurement Equivalents

1 Pint	= 16 Fluid Ounces	= 2 Cups
1 Quart	= 32 Fluid Ounces	= 2 Pints
1 Gallon	= 128 Fluid Ounces	= 4 Quarts

Converting Temperatures

Convert degrees Fahrenheit (F) to degrees Celsius (C) by following this simple formula: Subtract 32 from the Fahrenheit temperature reading. Then, multiply that number by 5/9. For example, 77°F - 32 = 45. 45 × 5/9 = 25°C.

To convert degrees Celsius to degrees Fahrenheit, multiply the Celsius temperature reading by 9/5. Then, add 32. For example, 25°C × 9/5 = 45. 45 + 32 = 77°F.

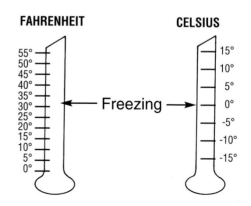

Contributors

Anchor Fence of Minnesota
7709 Pillsbury Avenue South
Richfield, MN 55423
(612) 866-4961

Buechel Stone Corp.
W3639 Hwy. H
Chilton, WI 53014-9643
(800) 236-4473
www.buechelstone.com

Cultured Stone Corporation
P.O. Box 270
Napa, CA 94559-0270
(800) 255-1727
www.culturedstone.com

Interlock Concrete Products Inc.
3535 Bluff Dr.
Jordan, MN 55352-8302
(800) 780-7212
www.interlock-concrete.com

International Masonry Institute
275 Market St # 511
Minneapolis, MN 55405
(800) 464-0988
www.imiweb.org

Pittsburgh Corning Corporation
800 Presque Isle Drive
Pittsburgh, PA 15239
(800) 624-2120
www.pittsburghcorning.com

The Quikrete Companies
2987 Clairmont Rd.
Suite 500
Atlanta, GA 30329
(800) 282-5828
www.quikrete.com

Warner Manufacturing Company
13435 Industrial Park Blvd.
Minneapolis, MN 55441
(800) 444-0606
www.warnertool.com

Hedberg Aggregates
1205 Nathan Lane North
Plymouth, MN 55441
(612) 545-4400
www.shadeslanding.com/
hedberg/

Other Resources

Brick Institute of America
11490 Commerce Park Drive,
Suite 300
Reston, VA 20191
(703) 620-0010
www.brickinfo.org

National Concrete
Masonry Association
P.O. Box 781
2302 Horse Pen Road
Herndon, VA 20171
(703) 713-1900
www.ncma.org

Portland Cement Association
5420 Old Orchard Road
Skokie, IL 60077
(847) 966-6200
www.portcement.org

Photo Credits

Crandall & Crandall
Dana Point, CA
© Crandall & Crandall – p. 138

Charles Mann
Santa Fe, NM
© Charles Mann – p. 91a

Jerry Pavia
Bonner's Ferry, ID
© Jerry Pavia – pp. 8a, 100a, 116,
139a, 139b

Michael S. Thompson
Eugene, OR
© Michael S. Thompson – p. 139c

*Licensing information for brick pavers
shown on page 64: UNI-Decor is a
registered trademark of F. von Langs-
dorff Licensing Ltd., Toronto, Ontario.
Symetry is a registered trademark of
Symrah Licensing Incorporated,
Cincinnati, Ohio.

Glossary

Adobe — sun-dried clay bricks commonly used in the southwestern United States.

Aggregate — materials such as sand, gravel, and crushed stone used to add strength to concrete and mortar, or to add traction to concrete surfaces.

Air entrainment — the addition of ingredients that cause bubbles to form in wet concrete and mortar, improving workability and frost resistance.

Ashlar — symmetrical stones typically used to lay up walls, pillars, and other vertical structures; also used to refer to patterns that rely on the use of ashlar stone.

Backfill — soil or rubble used as fill behind masonry construction.

Batter — a receding upward slope of the outer face of a wall or other structure; also called batter rate.

Batter gauge — a wooden device (typically homemade) used for gauging the slope of the sides of a vertical structure (see also *Batter*).

Bed joint — a horizontal joint in a masonry structure.

Bituminous felt — fiber strips saturated with asphalt; used to form expansion joints in a concrete slab for a patio, sidewalk, or driveway.

Bleed water — a thin layer of water that appears on some concrete mixtures after placement and must be permitted to dry before the concrete is worked.

Bonding agent — a coating designed to facilitate bonding between mortar and an existing surface.

Building paper — asphalt-impregnated paper used as a vapor barrier between wood or other sheathing and an outer surface, such as brick or stone veneer.

Bull float — a large, flat tool made of aluminum, magnesium, or wood; used for smoothing large slabs of freshly poured concrete.

Buttering — the process of using a trowel to place a contoured layer of mortar on a brick or other masonry unit before placement.

Capstone — the top stone or row of stones on a wall, pillar, or other vertical structure.

Cement — (see *Portland cement*).

Cobblestone — small cuts of quarried stone or fieldstone; often used in walks and paths.

Concrete — a combination of sand and gravel or crushed stone, held together by cement and water.

Construction joint — a contoured edge added to a portion of a concrete slab, designed to facilitate bonding when a pour must be interrupted.

Control joint — a joint in a concrete slab created by a control jointer or similar tool; designed to regulate cracking.

Darby — a long tool used for leveling and smoothing freshly poured concrete.

Dressing — the process of removing sharp points or protuberances on the exposed face of a stone, using a stone chisel and maul.

Dry mix — any packaged mix (typically sold in bags) that can be combined with water to form concrete, mortar, stucco, or masonry repair material.

Edger — a hand tool used for producing smooth edges on concrete slabs.

Efflorescence — deposits of salts that form after rising to the surface on masonry surfaces.

Expansion joint — also known as an isolation joint; a strip of bituminous felt separating sections of a concrete slab, or between new and old concrete; designed to allow for independent movement during freeze-thaw cycles.

Face — the exposed surface of a stone in masonry construction.

Field brick — one of multiple bricks that form the interior area of a wall, patio, driveway, or other surface.

Fieldstone — a type of stone typically collected from fields, riverbeds, or hillsides, often weather-worn in appearance; used with minor trimming in masonry construction; often used to refer to cobblestones or boulders with a similar appearance.

Finishing — the final texturing steps in masonry work, including leveling, edging, and smoothing joints.

Fire brick — a brick made with heat-resistant *fire clay* for use in fireplaces, chimneys, barbecues, and other high heat applications.

Fireclay mortar — any mortar to which fireclay has been added; now widely substituted with *refractory mortar,* which is less apt to disintegrate when exposed to high temperatures.

Flagstone — quarried stone cut into slabs usually less than 3 in. thick; used in walks, steps, and patios. Pieces smaller than 16" sq. are often called steppers.

Float — a metal or wood tool used on freshly poured concrete to produce a smooth and level surface (known as *floating*).

Floating — the technique of using a *float* to smooth and level freshly poured concrete.

Footing — a below-grade poured-concrete structure designed to support masonry and resist shifting.

Form — a wood or metal frame used for establishing the borders of a masonry project (usually poured concrete) and for containing the concrete as it is poured.

Freeze-thaw cycles — seasonal temperature changes that result in shifting of masonry and other structures.

Frost heave — damage to concrete and other paving materials due to ground temperature changes (see also *Freeze-thaw cycles*).

Groover — a tool used for cutting control joints in concrete and other masonry surfaces.

Hypertufa — a masonry material containing peat moss, *portland cement,* and other materials, and used to make planters, birdbaths, and other garden accessories.

Kerf — one of a series of narrow cuts in a piece of lumber, allowing it to be bent to create a curved construction form.

Key — a concave or contoured surface in freshly poured concrete designed to create a mechanical bond with subsequent layers or batches of concrete.

Landscape fabric — fabric used to contain soil and other loose materials, while allowing water to penetrate; also a barrier to plant growth.

Load-bearing — supporting substantial weight or resisting pressures from *backfill.*

Masonry unit — a brick, paver, block, or stone designed for use in masonry construction.

Mortar — a masonry mixture, usually containing *portland cement* and sand, that is applied with a trowel and hardens to form a bond between masonry units.

Mortar box — a wooden or plastic box used for mixing mortar for masonry projects.

Mortar hawk — a hand-held board used to hold small quantities of mortar during brick or block construction projects.

Mudjacking — the process of pumping fresh concrete under a slab or other structure that has shifted due to frost heave, soil settling, erosion, or other factors.

Parging — the technique of applying a layer of mortar to the backs of stones or other veneer materials to maximize contact with the bonding surface.

Plumb — standing perfectly vertical.

Plumb bob — a device, typically consisting of a pointed weight on the end of a string, used for determining that a surface is *plumb*.

Pointing (see *Tuck-pointing*).

Polyethylene — a type of plastic used in rolled sheeting (typically 4 to 6 mils thick) and used as a vapor barrier under slabs and in other masonry applications.

Portland cement — a combination of silica, lime, iron, and alumina that has been heated, cooled, and pulverized to form a fine powder from which concrete, mortar, and other masonry products are made.

PVC — rigid plastic (polyvinyl chloride) material that is highly resistant to heat and chemicals. PVC pipes are sometimes used to maintain spacing between masonry units.

Refractory mortar — a masonry mortar capable of withstanding exposure to high temperatures; used in high heat areas, such as fireplaces, chimneys, and barbecues.

Release agent — a substance applied to forms to prevent poured concrete from bonding with forms as the concrete hardens.

Rowlock — a header brick or other masonry unit laid on edge.

Rubble — irregular pieces of quarried stone, usually with one split or finished face, that are widely used in wall construction; called *rip-rap* when used as irregular fill.

Screed board — also known as a screed; a tool used for *screeding.*

Screeding — the technique of spreading soil, sand, crushed stone, fresh concrete, or other materials evenly across a project site to form a smooth, level surface.

Story pole — a pole or board marked at equal intervals to indicate the positioning of individual masonry units and to gauge mortar joint thickness.

Stucco — a smooth masonry mortar, also called *portland cement plaster;* used to create a weather-resistant barrier over metal lath or masonry surfaces.

Surface bonding cement — a smooth water-resistant masonry mortar designed for use as a coating over brick or concrete block walls for cosmetic, structural, or damp-proofing purposes.

Tie stone — a long stone in a wall or other structure, used to add strength by spanning the width of the structure.

Tuck-pointing — Also called *pointing;* the technique of finishing or repairing mortar joints by adding stiff mortar once the initial batch has dried. In repair projects, loose mortar is first removed to provide a solid surface to which fresh mortar can bond.

Veneer — a material, such as brick or natural or manufactured stone, that is applied to exterior or freestanding walls for cosmetic purposes.

Wall tie — a corrugated metal tie used to link adjacent masonry units or wythes in a structure; also used to secure veneer materials to walls.

Weep-hole — a hole, usually located at the base of a masonry structure to provide drainage for water behind the structure.

Wythe — A section of a wall that is the width of one masonry unit.

INDEX

Creative Publishing international, Inc. offers a variety of how-to books.
For information write:
  Creative Publishing international, Inc.
  Subscriber Books
  5900 Green Oak Drive
  Minnetonka, MN 55343